OTHER BOOKS IN THE COGNITIVE STRATEGY TRAINING SERIES
EDITOR: MICHAEL J. PRESSLEY, UNIVERSITY OF MARYLAND

Textbooks and the Students Who Can't Read Them

A Guide to Teaching Content

Jean Ciborowski
Children's Hospital, Boston

BROOKLINE BOOKS

Library of Congress Cataloging-in-Publication Data

Ciborowski, Jean. 1949-
    Textbooks and the students who can't read them : a guide to teaching content / Jean Ciborowski.
       p.   cm. -- (Cognitive strategy training series)
    Includes bibliographical references and index.

    1. Content area reading -- United States. 2. Textbooks -- United States -- Readability. 3. Reading -- United States -- Remedial teaching. 4. Reading comprehension -- Study and teaching -- United States. I. Title. II. Series.
LB1050.455.C53 1992   92-31933
428.4'071'2--dc20   CIP

Sixth printing,2005.

Printed in U.S.A. by Daamen, Inc., West Rutland, VT.

Published by
BROOKLINE BOOKS
P.O. Box 381047
Cambridge, MA 02238-1047
(617) 868-0360

To order or request a catalog, call toll-free:
1-800-666-BOOK

To Jeri Dee, Lindsey Ann, Dana,
and the one and only,
Matthew

Contents

Preface

Textbooks continue to dominate the elementary, middle and secondary curriculum as the major instructional tool. This position of dominance, however, has left them wide open to intense scrutiny, particularly in these recent years of criticism of the instructional outcomes of public education. The concern with textbooks has becomes particularly acute as educators have sought to place special education students in regular classes and maintain their learning productively.

But while researchers, curriculum experts, special interest groups, and special educators critique the nature of textbook content, the quality of instructional design and writing style, and indeed, what role the textbook should play in the larger curriculum, classroom teachers are faced with a more immediate dilemma: how to ignite their students' interests in the content and inspire them to read and study when so many lack the necessary skills to easily do so.

It is all too obvious that too many students have difficulty comprehending the materials presented in the textbooks intended for their use. To make matters worse, textbook content is often organized in such a way that the task of reading and thinking about them is made unduly difficult, particularly for the student with low reading skills. *It has also become clear that assigning reading, lecturing, and then asking questions is an ineffective way to teach them.*

This book proposes two major shifts in the way we think about low readers and textbook learning:

1. Students, even those with low reading skills, can learn to use the mainstream textbooks more effectively, and

2. textbooks can be designed to make them more usable not only for low readers, but for all students.

Toward this end, this book describes two novel practices for content teachers and special or remedial educators to consider. It presents:

1) a series of instructional techniques that teachers can use to improve their students' understanding of mainstream textbooks, particularly those students with low reading skills, and

2) ways to sharpen teachers' textbook consumer skills when selecting and purchasing textbooks for an increasingly diverse population of readers.

The instructional techniques described in Chapter 4 are designed to give teachers, especially those tired of the standardized textbook instruction, new ideas about ways to teach content.

In the last chapter, Chapter 5, are suggestions for teachers to use when examining textbooks for adoption—the pages are laid out so the teacher can photocopy those pages and take notes for each suggested criterion as they evaluate a textbook program for adoption.

The focus of this book, then, is on helping teachers make textbooks more understandable and usable by their students.

The process has three phases. Teachers must do more to prepare students for learning, and then help them integrate the new learning into what they already know. This approach requires teachers to rethink how they teach subject matter content to all students, but particularly to those who do not easily or fluently read the passages independently, or who learn the materials in different ways. The approach also requires teachers to make shifts in their thinking about how students learn.

Indeed, many of the strategies may seem to move teachers away from the textbook to the use of more relevant and interesting instructional tasks. The textbook comes to be viewed as a reference, a resource and a "training ground" for the act of reading, but its use does not dominate the teaching and learning processes.

The three phases are explained in the next chapter and presented in greater detail in Chapter 4.

Chapter 5 provides teachers with a means to critically evaluate the textbooks they consider for use in their classrooms. Ultimately, with more sensitivity to the elements which make user-friendly textbooks, teachers and school districts can make user-friendly textbooks begin to appear. The principles embodied in the three-step process will still apply, especially for the students who read textbooks with difficulty.

The methodology is not a rigid one. And while it adapts easily to meet individual teacher and student needs and strengths, its implementation is made much easier when the textbook is a good one. A good textbook is not overwhelmingly long, it is well written, and well organized.

We believe teachers of low readers must not only participate on textbook adoption committees, but they must become more critically aware of the nature of textbook organization, and how they might be organized to become more user-friendly to the teacher *and* the student, especially the students with reading difficulties. The suggestions later in the book are intended to help teachers sharpen their consumer skills so they can make better selections for all their students.

Jean Ciborowski
The Children's Hospital
Boston MA

CHAPTER 1

The Context for This Book: Improving Students' Understanding of Textbook Content

1. Instructional Techniques Designed to Improve Textbook Usability

Mrs. Romaine's fourth grade class is about to begin the next lesson on the Jamestown colony. She leads a lively discussion about the hardships encountered by the colonists and begins calling on her students to read orally from their textbooks. Six of her students are "dreading" to be called upon, for they are the ones who read painfully slowly, who stumble and stall on words, unable to fully grasp the meaning of what they read. Because these students have not yet acquired the proficiency of "learning-to-read," "reading-to-learn" from their textbook is overwhelmingly difficult.

***

Richard, an eighth-grader, has received academic support in the resource room for four years, but finds a 9-page U.S. history homework reading assignment exceedingly difficult. Too many of the words are unfamiliar, rendering the text incomprehensible. He skips ahead to the assigned chapter questions and attempts a random search for the answers with thoughts of only "getting it done." Lacking both confidence and interest, he completes the assignment poorly. Unprepared for the next day's class discussion, he avoids making eye contact with his teacher and prays he won't be called upon to participate. Unknowingly, he digs himself deeper into a "learning rut."

Students who are behind their peers in textbook reading do not need "watered down" textbooks, nor do they need "different" or "slower" instruction. Rather, they need instructors to help them discover **how** to regain the confidence in their abilities and the control of their learning lost through an accumulation of academic frustrations and failures. Toward this end, teachers must learn how to compensate for poor books and maximize good books when teaching the students who, as eighth-grade Richard and the fourth graders in Mrs. Romaine's class, do not learn in the expected ways.

The first way this can be achieved is through specific instructional techniques that are woven into the three distinct but recursive phases of teaching and learning. It is important to note that the phases do not segment teaching and learning content into easier parts and pieces, but are techniques that help students connect and expand concepts in their reading, writing and thinking behaviors.

For the student with low reading skills, the most critical phase is Phase I (Before Reading) because it is rooted strongly in the belief that **all** students have a reservoir of knowledge and experiences that can be utilized as a way to "prep" them for textbook learning. Once students feel their prior knowledge is seriously recognized and valued, they can begin to see the connections between their unique experiences and what they are learning. Feeling empowered, low readers can slowly regain the confidence to learn and invent strategies for organizing and integrating the textbook content into what they already know.

Phases II and III (During and After Reading) are opportunities for instructors to challenge their low readers as seriously as they challenge their good readers. And once teachers learn to teach strategies for comprehending, studying and consolidating the dramas, events and phenomena found in the history, social studies and sciences textbooks, they may find that even those students once thought to be disinterested can discover new reasons for reading, grow in the capacity to think critically and develop more positive attitudes toward school and learning.

Choosing Well-Designed Textbook Programs

A second way to improve the usability of textbooks for all students, but particularly low readers, is to select textbooks that give teachers choices and guidance about how to simultaneously teach reading, thinking and content, and activities that are rooted in principles of effective instruction.

Teachers can learn to sharpen their textbook consumer skills by considering textbook programs that meet the following four broad criteria:

- First, textbook programs (teacher materials) should emphasize the importance of connecting learning to student experience and igniting student interest by **including specific pre-reading activities that will get students "wanting to read."**

- Second, textbook programs (teacher materials) should prioritize the teaching of comprehension, thinking and content *concurrently.*

- Third, textbook programs (teacher materials) should describe novel assessment practices to give teachers new ideas about ways that help students consolidate "new" (textbook) knowledge with existing knowledge. Importantly, programs should "mark" content that lends itself to learning situations that can increase the chances of students feeling empowered (rather than defeated), becoming team problem-solvers (rather than loners), and active invested learners (rather than passive and apathetic).

- Fourth, the writing style of the student edition should not be contrived, stilted or dull; rather it should be a model of good writing, appealing and well organized, and include text features that can enhance rather than hinder reading comprehension.

CHAPTER 2

The Impetus for Change: The Students, The Textbooks, The Instruction

STUDENTS WHO CAN'T READ

According to the United States Department of Education (1991), the number of students placed in programs for specific learning disabilities has grown by 1,256,007 or 160 percent since 1976. During the school year 1989-1990, 2,064,892 children and youth were served in learning disability programs throughout the nation. Add to this number another broadly heterogeneous group of students referred to as *at risk* presumably because they are in danger of dropping out of school before graduation, or graduating without the necessary basic skills. While the significant increase of students identified as having learning problems continues to fuel debates about the definition of such terms as *specific learning disability* and *underachievement* and how best to treat these conditions, the fact remains that most of this population is plagued by problems in reading (Stanovich, 1986; National Center for Education Statistics, 1989; U.S. Dept. of Education, 1991).

Together these two groups constitute a sizeable number of students, many of whom have been placed in separate education programs, e.g., Chapter 1 or Special Education, in the hopes they will receive more appropriate instruction. In spite of these special programs, these students continue to find learning from their social studies, history and science textbooks overwhelmingly difficult. Discouraged by early reading failures and frustrations, feelings of defeat and helplessness are common when they confront the unfamiliar words and ambiguities in their textbooks. It is not surprising therefore that these students not only fail to "invent" efficient strategies for reading and studying, but fail to develop the motivation necessary to want to "learn more" from books.

Why Some Students Don't Learn to Read

More than likely, the students who experience problems reading their textbooks encountered difficulty when learning to read in the early grades. Growing evidence supports the notion that for the young child, the most critical factor in forming the necessary building blocks of reading is phonological awareness (Chall, 1983; Haskell, Foorman, & Swank, 1992; Stanovich, 1986a; Vellutino, 1991). Typically, this "awareness" develops during the first grade, allowing the child to discover how the letter-sound relationships are used to decode the printed word. Once the beginning reader can decode words both quickly and accurately, a level of "automaticity" is achieved that, in turn, facilitates reading fluency. Feeling gratified, the child is more likely to engage in "reading-practice" so that speed and accuracy continue to increase. Like a train leaving the station, slowly mounting speed and power, the beginning reader accumulates enough successes to travel down the track toward increasingly satisfying reading experiences.

Unfortunately, for reasons which are not entirely clear, some children do not develop the necessary phonological awareness. As a result, they are unable to experience the intrinsic gratification that spurs reading speed and accuracy. Instead, for these children, early reading experiences are stressful and defeating. They stay stuck on a stalled or painfully slow moving train acutely aware of their classmates moving past them with apparent ease.

For the child stuck in the early stages of reading, other areas of academic development will also suffer. Not only are spelling and writing skills intimately related to reading skills, the struggling reader will also be denied the opportunity to expand his or her knowledge base and vocabulary through reading experiences (Snider & Tarver, 1987). Presumably, what begins as a highly specific reading disability, therefore, interferes with the growth of other literacy areas. Ultimately, early reading difficulties spiral out of control, negatively affecting a child's ability to manage more conceptually dense materials such as the expository text found in textbooks. **Because these children have not learned to read efficiently, reading to learn from their textbooks is overwhelmingly difficult**. As they move up in the grades, many never catch up to their peers. As the gap between what they **can** read and what they **should** read continues to widen, learning and reading problems become more generalized, compromising word attack skills, comprehension and thinking strategies, attention, and sadly, self-esteem. The train never acquires quite enough steam, invariably slows down and may even slide backwards.

The Matthew Effect

As poor readers spend less time reading and are exposed to less "text" than their normal reading counterparts, they are unable to benefit from reading practice. To make matters worse, poor readers often receive a qualitatively different kind of instruction than good readers. Instead of engaging in reading of connected text, poor readers are spending more time on isolated skill work, workbooks, phonic sheets or other de-contextualized tasks. Exposed to less appealing and stilted text, the poor reader's problem is exacerbated while the good reader's reading gets better. Stanovich (1986) named this phenomenon "The Matthew Effect" from the gospel according to Matthew (XXV:29), which reads:

> For unto every one that hath shall be given, and he shall have abundance: but from him that hath not shall be taken away even that which he hath.
>
> (Stanovich, 1986a, p.318)

By the time these students are old enough for textbook learning, they may be unable to concentrate well when reading, appear easily distracted or anxious, particularly when called upon to read orally in front of their classmates. They may make careless errors, or fail to reflect carefully before answering a question, instead "jumping in" with an impulsive guess. They are anxious and uncertain about their reading ability and their uncertainty or anxiety generalizes to other learning tasks. Students appear "passive," beaten down by the feelings of defeat that come from the cumulative effects of years of frustrations and failures in reading. Not surprisingly, they are often ill-equipped with strategies for organizing their materials and studying for tests. They seem to lack awareness of their learning style (i.e, their error-patterns, their limitations, their strengths) and the demands of the task at hand. As a result, these students tend to "plod" through the textbook reading assignment, rarely re-reading or self-questioning when they are confused or in doubt of a word or meaning.

By this time in students' academic life, their perceptions of their social competence can also be wielding considerable influences on achievement. Social experiences can weigh heavily upon the students' feelings of competence and their perceptions of others' expectations of their skills both in and out of the classroom. Students can have feelings and beliefs that can negatively affect their willingness to risk socially or academically—offering possibly incorrect answers, to persevere on a task, to be comfortable about their social desirability to others, and problem-solving behaviors in both academic and social settings. Clearly, the cumulative and reverberating effects of the school failure can not only suffocate a desire to read, but hamper the development of intrinsic motivation to learn and pursue school-based interests (sometimes most interests), and a positive attitude toward school and learning more generally. It is not surprising that these students feel little control over their own ability to learn in the school setting. *** *Figure 2-1*

Successful textbook learning, then, is a complex and coordinated interaction of numerous factors which influence learning and reading:

First, reading fluency, i.e., recognizing high frequency words easily and the ability to decode less familiar words, must be sufficiently developed so that the reader can successfully grapple with new words and other ambiguities he/she confronts in textbook reading.

Second, consistent levels of attention, reflection and strategies for organizing and remembering information must develop.

Figure 2-1
Contrasting READING Characteristics

Students With Learning Problems	Students Who Do Well in School
Struggle with the transition from learning-to-read to reading-to-learn.	Make the transition smoothly from
Have difficulty paying attention; may get distracted easily	Maintain consistent levels of attention
Passive learner; construct fewer efficient learning strategies	Active learners; construct efficient learning strategies
Accumulated feelings of failure effects motivation to learn more	Are motivated to learn more; have experienced academic success
Feel little control over their learning	Have a sense of control of their learning

Third, a self-awareness must develop so readers will be able to know when they are comprehending *and* when they are "feeling" confused. This awareness (metacognition) allows readers to proceed and/or adjust the way they interact with the text, e.g., reread the line of text, ask "silent" questions of themselves about text, make mental or actual notes about salient ideas, and so forth.

Fourth, a self-motivating sense of competence and control is necessary for readers to want to learn from their textbooks or from any other reading materials.

THE INDOMITABLE TEXTBOOK

The method of using textbooks to teach is rooted in strong social and pedagogical traditions. Parents like to see their children learning from textbooks, and during the 1980's they became increasingly active in the process of appraising and adopting textbooks in their local school systems. Parent groups began to pressure schools not only to cover certain topics in certain ways, but also to teach more content areas, pushing schools to present more and more information to be learned in a short amount of time.

Teachers, too, place a high value on the textbook as an indispensable instructional tool. Studies estimate that students spend as much as 75 percent of their classroom time and 90 percent of their homework time involved with textbook material (Woodward & Elliot, 1990), and that dependence upon textbooks increases with grade level (Goodlad, 1976).

While textbooks remain unchallenged in their role as the primary instructional tool, they have, in recent years, been the focus of repeated controversy (see: J.D. Herlihy, (Ed.),1992, *The Textbook Controversy*). Among other things, textbooks have been criticized for decreasing difficulty (Chall & Conard, 1991), stilted writing (Tyson-Bernstein, 1988; Britton, 1988), covering too much information in too little depth, avoiding controversy (Chall, Conard, & Harris,1977; Gagnon, 1986; Larkins & Hawkins, 1987; Tyson-Bernstein & Woodward, 1989;) and poor instructional design (Armbruster & Gudbrandsen, 1986; EDC, RMC Corporation, 1989). As a result, critics argue that today's textbooks fail to do their part in

1) motivating students to read more about a topic,

2) influencing the development of comprehension and problem solving skills and

3) helping students to engage in higher order critical thinking.

It comes as no surprise therefore that textbook flaws serve to make reading that much more difficult for the student with poor skills.

Two Different Kinds of "Text"

Social studies, history and science textbooks are written in expository text. Unlike narrative text which has a "story" format, expository text is characterized by a variety of formats or structures depending upon the content. The concept map below shows the difference between the two types of text.

Understanding the differences between expository and narrative text helps us understand why some children have difficulty reading textbooks. Children are fed a steady diet of once-upon-a time stories during the infant, toddler and learning-to-read years, and so become increasingly familiar with the format and structures of narrative text. Familiarity with story text format makes comprehension easier. On the other hand, expository text is less familiar to the child in both content and format. Expository text structures differ dramatically from narrative text, including more varied and complex structures such as comparisons, contrasts, causes and effects, and problems and solutions. At the same time, the content of expository text is filled with many words and concepts the child has never seen before.

When textbooks are introduced in third and fourth grades, many children are caught by surprise, unprepared to make the transition from learning-to-read from stories to reading-to-learn from textbooks (Thrope, 1986). And, since reading comprehension is influenced by the prior knowledge the reader has "built up" from informal learning experiences and previous reading experiences, a major question especially for teachers of low readers is how features of expository text, impede or facilitate comprehension in young readers.

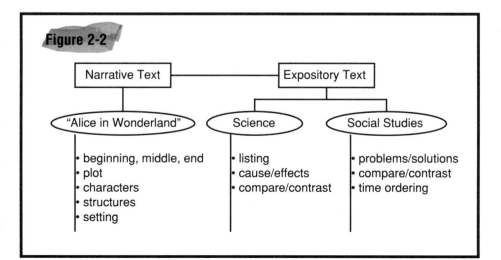

Figure 2-2

| Narrative Text | Expository Text |

| "Alice in Wonderland" | Science | Social Studies |

- beginning, middle, end
- plot
- characters
- structures
- setting

- listing
- cause/effects
- compare/contrast

- problems/solutions
- compare/contrast
- time ordering

How Features of a Textbook Can Influence Comprehension

A substantial amount of research has been conducted on the relationship between text organization and comprehension (Anderson & Armbruster, 1984; Armbruster, Osborne & Davison, 1985; Armbruster & Anderson, 1988). As one way to view how expository text is organized, Armbruster and her colleagues from the Center for the Study of Reading developed a model of a "considerate" textbook that involves three distinctive but interrelated features: *structure, coherence* and *audience appropriateness*.

Structure

Structure is a textbook feature that has to do with words, phrases and sentences which help cue the reader to upcoming information. *Explicit structure* is achieved when there is useful information for the reader in headings and subheadings, explicitly stated main ideas or topic sentences, clearly written chapter preview and summary statements, pointer words (i.e., first, second, third, etc.), and other signal words that make obvious the following possible relationships:

- a comparison or a contrast;
- a problem followed by a solution;
- a cause followed by an effect;
- a listing or a sequence of events.

Convincing evidence exists that when text is written so that the structures are made explicit, information is more accessible, and the reader is more likely to understand and remember what is read (Thorndyke, 1977; Loman & Mayer, 1983; Berkowitz, 1986; Gold & Fleisher, 1986).

Therefore, textbook reading is made more difficult for low readers when:

- main ideas are embedded or inferred;
- headings and subheadings are vague or ambiguous;

- chapter preview or summary statements are poorly written or do not exist.

Examples of Explicit and Implicit Structure

Explicit	Implicit
Useful Information in Headings	*Not-So-Useful Information in Headings*
• "John Smith's Life is Saved by Pocahontas"	• "A Stranger in America"
• "The Difficult Journey from England to Jamestown"	• "Jamestown"

Coherence

Coherence refers to how well ideas are integrated and flow within textbook lessons and across chapters and units. Coherence is achieved through a writing style characterized by explicit statements about the relationships among ideas, clear pronoun references, and references that support graphics. Coherence is important because coherent text is more understandable and therefore more meaningful. Unfortunately, many textbooks are written to readability formulas which adversely affect coherence (Armbruster, Osborne & Davison, 1985; Tyson-Bernstein & Woodward, 1989).

Therefore?. . . The text is rendered *less*, not more coherent and understandable for low readers when:

- textbook chapters have inconsistent writing styles; and
- sentences are shortened to conform to readability formulas thereby deleting important words (e.g., "however," "because," "in addition to," "such as," etc.). The writing becomes wooden, stilted and dull,

Example of Grade 5 Text Written to Readability Formula

"In 1608, Captain John Smith was chosen to be the leader of Jamestown. He ordered "He that will not work shall not eat." Everyone had to work in the fields. Smith became friends with the Powhatan Indians. The settlers began to trade with the Indians to get food. Things were getting better in Jamestown. But in 1609, Captain Smith was badly burned when his gunpowder exploded. He returned to England for medical help. By that time, 500 people were living in Jamestown. Things got worse after Smith left. The first winter without Smith was known as the "starving time."

Rewriting the Same Text Using More Explicit Structures and Coherence

In 1608, Captain John Smith was chosen to be the leader of the Jamestown Colony. As a leader, he believed in two important things: 1) everyone had to work very hard; and 2) everyone had to learn to get along with the Powhatan Indians. Smith was a good leader, but just when life was beginning to improve for the colony, his gunpowder accidentally exploded and he was forced to sail back to England to see his doctor. Unfortunately, after he left things got worse for the colony. Conditions became so bad that the first winter without Smith was known as "The Starving Time."

Audience Appropriateness

The third textbook feature, **audience appropriateness,** refers to the match between the text and the reader's level of knowledge and skill. *When students are reading well, they are reading and thinking simultaneously.* They are able to do this by accessing ideas from their preexisting knowledge that, in turn, enables them to make more sense of the words and phrases, and predict the upcoming meaning in the text. Therefore, when textbooks are *audience appropriate* they convey concepts in such a way that the reader's prior and relevant knowledge is activated. This can be done in three ways:

1) meaty (vs. superficial) explanations of the topic

2) the use of analogies to explain complicated or abstract ideas, and

3) the use of "friendly talk" or meta-discourse (talking directly to the reader by using the pronoun "you").

Therefore. . . textbook **learning is made** more difficult for low readers when:

- too many topics are treated too superficially; and
- the text lacks words or phrases that help activate reader's prior knowledge.

Considerate **textbooks can facilitate comprehension. Students with low reading skills need** *considerate* **textbooks.**

THE INSTRUCTION

Efforts to address problems students encounter when reading textbooks can be traced to writings as far back as the beginning decades of the twentieth century. The method was referred to as "teaching reading and content simultaneously," and was the result of a far-sighted recognition that students need certain strategies to manage different kinds of text (see: Moore, Readence & Rickelman, 1983, for a discussion of this method's historical context).

Essentially, the practice of teaching reading and content simultaneously involved students in very specific "active" reading activities that presumably enhanced their understanding of content and ultimately improved their academic performance. Reading activities that occurred before students were asked to read the content materials were thought to arouse and stimulate the reader's interest. The idea reemerged with the publication of a number of textbooks devoted to the topic, including Herber's "Teaching Reading in the Content Areas" (1978); Lunstrum and Taylor's "Teaching Reading in the Social Studies (1980); Readence, Bean and Baldwin's "Content Area Reading" (1981); Vacca's "Content Area Reading" (1981), and more recently, Irwin's "Reading and the Middle School Student" (1989), and Santa and Alvermann's "Science Learning: Processes and Applications' (1991), to name only a few.

Contemporary educators, however, have been slow to adopt this practice. **One reason for the resistance to integrate reading** and content instruction appears to be that many content teachers believe that reading instruction is not their responsibility, and that special education or remedial programs in reading are available to meet the needs of those students with poor reading skills (Gee & Forester, 1988).

Unfortunately, a closer look at the effectiveness of special programs designed to help students with "specific learning and reading disabilities" reveals a troubling picture. While the intent of Chapter I and the Education for All Handicapped Children Act of 1975 (Public Law, 94-142) was to create more "appropriate" educational programs for handicapped and "low achieving" students, evaluations of special education and Chapter I programs have not produced the expected benefits (Bloomer, Bates, Brown, & Norlander, 1982; Stainback & Stainback, 1987; Slavin, Karweit, & Madden, 1989; Fourqurean & LaCourt, 1990; Zigmond, 1990; Bartnick & Parkay, 1991).

One explanation for special education's disappointing track record may have to do with the failure of its policies and practices about educating children and youth with learning problems in reflecting two important notions. **First, all children and youth have strengths and successfully problem solve in areas other than school where they feel more confident and competent.** Past approaches in teaching, however, have not taken students' strengths seriously into account and failed to use them to build bridges to new learning. Instead, instructional approaches have remained stubbornly fixed on students' *disabilities* rather than students' *abilities*. **Second, policies and practices have been slow to reflect what we have learned about the development of learning and reading in children and reinforce the misconception that the learning problem resides exclusively within the child.** As practitioners insist on "focusing" on the deficiency, the strong influences of the child's social culture, the quality of instruction and the quality of instructional materials on learning and achievement are too often ignored. Indeed, a common special education practice is not to integrate reading instruction and content instruction, but rather to separate them. And too often the practice fails because it breaks apart what is inextricably linked: the content and the reading strategies necessary for learning it.

Policies and practices that break learning down into parts and pieces are rooted in reductionist theories of learning. Rather than describing learning as a generative, connected process of constructing, expanding and extending new knowledge, reductionist thinkers segment learning into skills and objectives to be mastered and met over a certain amount of time in a certain order. (See Poplin, 1988, for an excellent review of the effects of reductionist thinking on special education policies and practices).

As these misconceptions remained unchallenged, separate curricula, separate classrooms and separate teachers are created in an attempt to "fix" the problem learner. This practice of "separating" results in fragmented learning experiences, and ultimately less professional accountability for the progress of these students by dispersing responsibility for teaching them (Reynolds, Wang & Walberg, 1987; McGill-Franzen & Allington, 1991). However, even as it becomes increasingly clear that our current instructional models of instruction are sorely outdated, low achievers and learning handicapped students continue to fail and drop out of school at an alarmingly high rate. (According to an 1989 review of dropout studies, the rate is as high as 50 percent; see Wolman, Bruininks and Thurlow, 1989).

Unfortunately, no clear course of direction in either policy or pedagogy has been agreed upon to fortify educators in facing this growing problem. Content instructors are caught in a particularly difficult bind, because as they face more heterogeneous classrooms in which the reading skills among their students may span several years, they are still held accountable for raising test scores and covering an enormous amount of material in a short amount of time. And although differences in the way students learn have become better understood, they are not easily accommodated, particularly when classrooms are large, resources are limited and, in many cases, shrinking.

As a result, there is a growing belief that special and regular educators must pool their resources and work **collaboratively** in educating these students more effectively (Bruce & Chan, 1991; Idol, West & Lloyd, 1988; Will, 1986). Collaborative teaching means that general and special educators negotiate around what and how to teach the content, as well as determine which instructional setting (i.e., resource room, content classroom, after, school study session), is the best place to introduce and review learning strategies.

Pioneers in the research of effective instruction have demonstrated viable ways to work with low readers in the content classroom. In fact, several methodologies have been successful in helping low readers with comprehension and textbook learning in the general education setting.

For example, reciprocal teaching (Palinscar & Brown, 1984, 1986, 1988), is particularly promising because it is based upon an understanding of the developmental nature of learning and reading, as well as an appreciation for the widening diversity among readers' prior learning experiences. By emphasizing a collaboration between students and teacher in constructing meaning from the text, low readers are continually placed in positions to feel more control of their learning, thereby acquiring more confidence in their ability to learn.

A second methodology, strategy training (Deshler & Schumaker, 1986; Harris & Pressley, 1991; Lovitt & Horton, 1991; Pressley, 1990; Pressley, El-Dinary, Gaskins, Schuder, Bergman, Alamasi & Brown, 1992) assumes that students can be taught similar knowledge, beliefs and behaviors that are observed in students who do well in the classroom. Strategy training begins by securing teacher, student and administrative commitment, so that carefully planned long-term instruction in strategic thinking, reading, and problem solving can be integrated into the core curricula.

A third methodology is cooperative learning. Cooperative learning involves groups of students with varying abilities who work collaboratively toward a common goal. Cooperative learning has been successful, particularly for students who have experienced learning difficulties, because the pressure to succeed shifts from the individual student to the group. Students feel less isolated when working or reading in groups, and therefore less frightened of failure.

And bigger changes are proposed by reformers who seek to restructure the curriculum so that students who have experienced a history of school failures participate more fully in the design and implementation of the curriculum (e.g., The Foxfire Pedagogy: Ensminger & Dangel, 1992).

Given the primary role the textbook continues to play in teaching and learning, the increasing student diversity and widening range of reading skills among students in social studies, history and science classrooms, **the question becomes how to best help students with low reading skills learn from their textbooks.**

It was in this spirit of educational reform that the U.S. Department of Education, Office of Special Education, called upon educators, researchers and publishers to collaborate in improving the usability of textbooks for students with learning and reading disabilities, particularly those students "mainstreamed" in general education content classrooms. Education Development Center (EDC) in Newton, Massachusetts, and RMC Research Corporation in Hampton, New Hampshire, collaborated on an 18-month project to improve the usability of textbooks by training teachers to analyze the 12 most commonly used social studies, history and science textbook programs. The findings of this study, as well as the recommendations to educational publishers, are discussed in the next chapter.

CHAPTER 3

An Analysis of 12 Textbook Programs*

In 1985, with funding from the U.S. Department of Education, Office of Special Education, Education Development Center (EDC) in Newton Massachusetts, and RMC Research Corporation in Hampton, New Hampshire, undertook a project to improve textbooks for students experiencing learning problems. The project involved a qualitative analysis of 12 widely used social studies and science textbook programs. It culminated in a national conference for teachers, publishers and researchers in Washington D.C.(EDC and RMC Corp, 1989). (See Appendix A for the list of textbooks analyzed and a summary of the study methodology.)

In order to draw upon teachers' "first hand" experiences with textbooks and students, four elementary and four secondary teachers were recruited to conduct the appraisals of the twelve textbook programs. The textbook appraisers were teachers of science, social studies or history whose classes included students with learning handicaps. Teachers agreed to commit at least 100 hours to training and assessment activities beyond their teaching responsibilities, and were financially compensated for their time. Their initial findings were subsequently verified at a three-day conference by 40 additional content and special needs teachers.

In order to accomplish the appraisal task, it was necessary to examine three distinct components of the textbook program. The first component included the instructional techniques, typically discussed in the teacher's edition, supplemental instruction guidelines (e.g., teacher's resource packet, laboratory

* This chapter is adapted from (EDC and RMC Corp., *Final Report, Improving Textbook Usability*, Newton, MA.: Education Development Center. ERIC Reproduction Number ED 303 934.

guide, etc.), or in suggested individualized activities for special learners. The second component included the actual student materials, primarily the student's textbook but also included workbooks, enrichment activities, and tests. Finally, the appraisal addressed the integrity of the whole program, and attempted to elicit a profile of broad strengths and weaknesses of the textbook program.

The teacher-reviewers were not asked to examine content. Although its importance and significant relationship to the instructional design was acknowledged, content evaluation was clearly beyond the scope of the project's mission. An assumption was made, however, that a well-designed textbook program (i.e., pedagogically sound instructional strategies and "considerate" textbook features) did not have to compromise content.

The teacher reviewers did not determine readability. The use of readability formulas impedes the effort to improve the quality of writing. As helpful connecting words are excluded to conform to formula, sentences are shortened and simplified, and writing is made stilted, dull and less comprehensible. Moreover, readability formulas fail to take into account key factors that affect comprehension: the organization of ideas, the author's writing style, the page layout, the motivation, interest and prior knowledge of the reader (Armbruster, Osborne & Davison, 1985).

What teacher reviewers did do was search for 1) principles of effective instruction known to work well with students with learning problems such as: reciprocal teaching techniques, collaborative learning approaches, direct instruction of learning strategies and peer tutoring approaches and 2) text features that enhance comprehension.

It was during this process the teacher reviewers experienced a major shift in their thinking about the needs of low readers and textbook learning.

What Teachers Said About Textbooks and Low Readers

At the completion of the long appraisal process, teachers reported their initial impressions.

Figure 3-1
The Teacher-Appraisers' Shift in Viewing the Needs of Low Readers

From	*To*
Children make the transition between learning-to-read to reading-to-learn (from their textbooks) easily and smoothly.	Some beginning textbook users need help in making the transition between learning-to-read and reading-to-learn.
Reading has been mastered by the time a student uses his/her textbook.	Reading and thinking must occur simultaneously with teaching content.
Textbook readers "automatically" know how to comprehend, remember and study from their textbooks.	Teachers must model HOW to comprehend, remember and study from a textbook.
Low readers will get the help they need in special education or remedial reading with a separate teacher and different textbook.	Low readers need integrated rather than fragmented instruction, and frequent practice of reading and writing of extended text.

- Many felt strongly that if textbooks were improved for students experiencing learning problems, the improvements would benefit **ALL** their students:

   "....what's good for students with learning problems would probably be good for all students."(Elementary Science Teacher)

- Others commented on the process itself and how they had learned to think about textbooks in a new way:

   ....."the process made us look at textbooks in a way we never would have done on our own." (Grade 6, Science Teacher)

- Other reviewers were struck by the **differences** in the quality of instructional activities for low and high achievers:

....." I found repeatedly — the books would talk about enrichment activities ... and they were kind of fun things— political cartoons or interviewing of people, things that really got kids involved. But these activities were reserved for achievers, and it's precisely these kinds of activities that are good for kids at any level. (Junior High Social Studies Teacher)

- Criticism was also raised against what the reviewers perceived as reinforcement of teacher-centered (vs. student-centered) instruction:

  "...The thing I found emphasized in the secondary social studies textbook was the lecture format, the talking head. The teacher is the talking head and kids sit as recorders ... little creativity on the teacher's part and none on the student's - just sit, read and write."

- When activities for the "special needs" students were reviewed, teachers reported that they seemed to be token attempts or add-ons, not well integrated with the chapter/ unit goals:

  ....."two or three suggestions were "added on" for special needs students, often for the visually or physically handicapped, but they didn't tie into the goals of the lesson." (Grade 6 Science Teacher)

- A frequent criticism was that secondary textbook programs did not do a good job in helping teachers determine the "core" or most important information, given the reality that all chapters will not be covered:

  "...nowhere does the book suggest what is most important to teach ... no one wants to say — that's why so many teachers do the stand-up format. There is so little time and so much material to cover. I found the best way to help students with learning difficulties is to pick {themes} they should learn and do lots of activities around the (theme). (Grade 8-11, History Teacher)

- Many teachers also commented on the lack of strategies to teach content as well as inconsistent attention to help students organize and recall substantial amounts of information. Publishers, they reported, had not kept up with the "mainstreaming" trend and had made too many incorrect assumptions about student as well as teacher needs:

> "...Only at the beginning of the book, it read [these are basic science skills that you need. Do before Chapter 1......] and then you don't do any more for the rest of year..!" (Grade 9 -12, Chemistry Teacher)

- And other teachers went on to say:

> "I don't want a textbook telling me what to do. You do this first, you do this second....But I would like to have as much information so I can pick and choose.." (Grade 6, Science Teacher)

> "Publishers should let us know what the prerequisite knowledge should be. Somewhere in the middle of the lesson, I read ...[and as you know] and I 'm thinking ...how should I know? And I realize that this fact was presented in the earlier chapter. Wouldn't it be nice if the teacher knew that before she or he decided not to teach that chapter?" (Grade 4, Social Studies Teacher)

- When teachers examined the treatment of vocabulary and key concepts, they were confused when they found that some "new" vocabulary words were highlighted and others were not; concepts were rarely introduced, much less explained:

> " ..The words they chose to highlight amazed me— words that kids probably already knew ...then there would be highly technical words they would not highlight." (Grade 6, Science Teacher)

- Furthermore, teachers felt that it was not easy to coordinate the various pieces of the textbook program (i.e., teacher's materials, student's material, ancillary materials) and that it was difficult to determine the relationships among all the many parts:

> "....sitting there with 9 pieces saying [do I do this first, or last, with which student?]" (Grade 9 -12, Chemistry Teacher)

- In terms of writing style, reviewers commented that some chapters were inconsistent in the style:

> "...There were chapters that felt like they had been written by a different author. The grouping was different, the

activities ... I had a sense that the words were different.."
(Grade 6, Science Teacher)

TEACHERS' FINAL ANALYSIS OF TEXTBOOK PROGRAMS

Together, the information compiled from the literature review, the initial textbook analyses and the verification process revealed a **general criticism of textbook programs for use with students experiencing learning problems or in the lowest quartile of the classroom.**

In terms of *instructional pedagogy*, four major conclusions were reached:

1. "For the most part, the textbook programs reviewed fell short in accommodating students with learning problems by failing to reflect effective methods of instruction. Rather, attempts to meet the needs of these students appeared as add-on "activities for special learners." **They were often isolated from the context, inappropriate or dull.**"

2. "Elementary books were rated better than secondary because they made more consistent attempts to integrate principles of effective instruction."

3. "Secondary programs seldom included important information about organizational, study or test-taking strategies. They generally did not provide teachers with creative ways for presenting content or evaluating student performances."

4. "Most programs were criticized for not emphasizing the importance of ongoing teacher evaluation. Books were inconsistent in providing teachers with guidance about checking prerequisite knowledge and skills and assessing students' misconceptions before proceeding."

(1989, EDC/RMC Final Report pp. 23-24)

In terms of *textbook features*, the student materials, three major conclusions were reached:

1. "In general, the textbook programs reviewed failed to integrate structural features known to facilitate comprehension, organization and recall."

2. "Secondary textbook programs were rated poorest in accommodating students with reading and other learning problems. They were too large and all-encompassing, poorly organized, and inconsistent in their uses of structures (e.g., explicit main ideas, useful information in headings and subheadings, clear statements of the problem/solution, cause/effect, well-written preview and summary statements, etc.).

3. "Textbook programs were rated fair in integrating features to enhance the reader's interest. Elementary books were inconsistent in their use of metadiscourse (or friendly talk), and secondary textbooks tended to have a stilted, unengaging writing style."

(1989, pp. 23, 24)

How Can Textbooks Be Better Designed?

The teachers' final appraisals of the textbooks were particularly critical because of their lack of accommodation for the increasing student diversity in classrooms today. **Given this reality, teachers were eager to learn ways to compensate for poor books and maximize good books when teaching students who do not learn in the expected ways.**

At the same time, teachers of students with low reading skills learned how to identify the less usable textbook programs from the more usable textbook programs. Subsequently, they formulated specific recommendations that educational publishers could use to improve the usability of social studies, history and science textbook programs.

Their recommendations were grounded in the assumption that low readers, in order to be more successful in learning from their textbooks, must be exposed to carefully planned phases of instruction: pre-reading, during reading and post-reading. Within each phase, the teachers recommended the following:

What Teachers of Low Readers Recommended to Textbooks Publishers

Teachers were in strong agreement that while average and above-average students often manage to do well without specific instruction on how to read their textbooks, low readers do not. Clearly, students with low reading skills need very specific guidance and instruction before reading, when they are engaged in sustained silent reading and once they have completed the reading assignment. Therefore, teacher reviewers argued that the textbook pedagogy must reflect the notion that teaching content consists of three interrelated processes or phases. Toward this end, they recommended to educational publishers:

1. **That in teacher materials**, there should be:

- more attention to focusing instruction

- more attention to the importance of tapping prior knowledge

- information on common student misconceptions and suggestions for addressing them

- more guidance about ways to teach students how to preview the text by using text structures [Phase I].

2. **That in teacher materials**, there should also be:

- specific suggestions as to how to teach comprehension monitoring strategies. For example, behaviors such as self-questioning, rereading, paraphrasing, predicting, and summarizing are ways readers can monitor when they are comprehending and when they are not.

- easy to read explanations of the various other kinds of strategies, (e.g., visual imagery strategies, memory strategies, organizational strategies, etc.) and how, when, and why they should be used;

- a designation of which chapters, lessons or ideas lend themselves well to teaching and learning strategies;

- guidance about cooperative learning structures (i.e., peer teaching, small group work, teamwork) and a designation of the content that lends itself to group problem solving activities. [Phase II].

3. **That in teacher materials**, there should also be:

- suggestions for evaluation other than traditional testing that foster higher order and critical thinking

- suggestions that require writing of extended text and activities that develop interest beyond the classroom and into students' homes and communities [Phase III].

At the completion of the project, 120 people, including the project teachers, educational publishers, scholars and others involved in textbook reform, met in Washington, D.C. to discuss the study findings. Not surprisingly, discussion focused on the best way to assess textbook usability. Questions were raised about how subject matter (social studies vs. science) and grade levels (elementary vs. secondary) should influence the design of a textbook analysis tool. Serious concerns were raised about the textbook adoption process and the forces for and against textbook reform. By the end of the conference, however, consensus was reached on the following three broad recommendations:

- more active collaboration is needed among teachers, educational publishers, and researchers at every stage of textbook development;

- more thinking is needed about the relationship between evaluation and effective textbook instruction and the role of the textbook in the larger curriculum;

- pre-service and in-service must include the study of the use of textbooks, the reading and strategy research and effective instruction for students who do not learn in the expected ways; understanding the relationship between learner and text characteristics is essential.

(*Conference Proceedings, Improving Textbook Usability*, 1989, Education Development Center, Inc., & RMC Research Corp., pp.36, 37).

In the meantime, as publishers make changes in textbooks in order to meet the evolving needs of the educational market, teachers have little choice but to use the textbooks available in their school system. And while some teacher surveys confirm that teachers are in fact happy with their books, still others find it difficult to use one textbook in a class with students of increasingly varying reading abilities.

The following chapter is designed for teachers who are looking for ways to make their existing textbooks more usable in a classroom of students whose reading levels may span several years.

CHAPTER 4

Using Textbooks With Low Readers

COLLABORATING INSTRUCTION: REGULAR AND SPECIAL EDUCATORS WORKING TOGETHER TO IMPROVE TEXTBOOK USABILITY

Many students with low reading skills are participating in special education, Chapter I or other kinds of remedial or tutorial programs. Therefore, it is **essential** that teachers be willing to collaborate with one another in working toward acquiring:

1) new knowledge and beliefs about teaching and the way children and youth learn;

2) effective teaching techniques to better meet the needs of a more diverse student population;

(For the content instructor)

3) **an appreciation for the developmental and connected nature of reading, thinking and *learning content*;**

(For the remedial or special needs instructor)

4) **an appreciation for the depth and breadth of the content needed to be covered**

Collaborating teachers must be good planners and must be able to set aside brief but regularly scheduled planning time. Administrative support for planning therefore is essential. When teachers from the different disciplines are encouraged to begin talking and problem solving together, a sense of camaraderie can develop. Together, amelioration of student failure can be addressed more quickly, and recognition for student achievement can be shared more equally.

COLLABORATIVE TEXTBOOK TEACHING

- must involve the student's special educator and content teachers meeting and planning on a regular basis;

- should include regular assessments of the needs of the students having difficulty;

- must emphasize the integration of content and learning and reading strategies;

- should encourage teachers to solicit feedback from one another about how they are doing.

If teachers pool their resources and talents to collaborate in making the teaching decisions on a regular basis, substantial benefits can be reaped for **all** students in the classroom as well:

The Content: What chapters will be covered?

In what order?

When will they be covered?

In what depth?

The Strategies: What strategies will be taught to learn this content?

How will they be taught?

In what setting? (i.e., resource room? learning center? content classroom?)

How will strategies be reinforced over time?

Who will teach them, or support those that are useful that students were taught?

In the event low readers do not participate in academic support programs, the content teacher must learn to implement the three-phase textbook teaching and learning model alone.

THE THREE-PHASE TEXTBOOK TEACHING AND LEARNING MODEL

The three phases of teaching and learning are generative and interconnected; Phase I prepares students for Phase II; which in turn prepares students for Phase III. Ideally, learning a lesson or a chapter is viewed as a thoughtful, well-planned construction of knowledge that continually undergoes the processes of rebuilding, readjusting, and extension of that knowledge.

What holds this mighty construction of knowledge together are the meaningful and logical connections between what has already been learned and experienced, and what is about to be learned in the textbook.

There is more to instructing low readers in the content area than preparing them to read their textbook. Indeed, specific guided reading and after-reading activities are also vital parts of the methodology.

Phase I: Before Reading: Giving Low Readers a "Head Start"

Phase II: During Reading: Getting Students to Become More Active Comprehenders and Thinkers While Reading

Phase III: After Reading: Getting Students to Consolidate and Extend Their Textbook Knowledge

The three-phase model is also based upon an understanding of the learner characteristics of low readers, and **how** they compare to good readers when engaged in textbook learning. A closer look at how the two groups compare in "before", "during" and "after" reading behaviors strongly suggests that **low readers are not prepared to begin reading from their textbooks**, and further, **tend not to possess the necessary reading strategies for efficient comprehension.** The chart below establishes a clear rationale for the three-phase instructional strategies which follow.

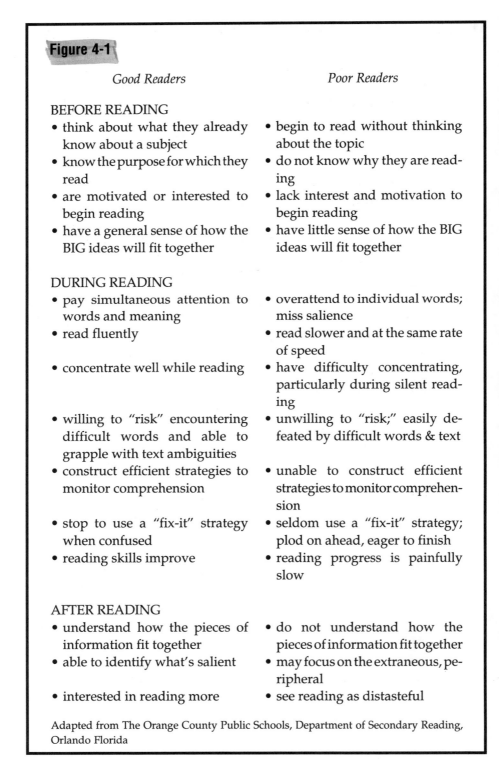

Figure 4-1

	Good Readers	*Poor Readers*

BEFORE READING

Good Readers	Poor Readers
• think about what they already know about a subject	• begin to read without thinking about the topic
• know the purpose for which they read	• do not know why they are reading
• are motivated or interested to begin reading	• lack interest and motivation to begin reading
• have a general sense of how the BIG ideas will fit together	• have little sense of how the BIG ideas will fit together

DURING READING

Good Readers	Poor Readers
• pay simultaneous attention to words and meaning	• overattend to individual words; miss salience
• read fluently	• read slower and at the same rate of speed
• concentrate well while reading	• have difficulty concentrating, particularly during silent reading
• willing to "risk" encountering difficult words and able to grapple with text ambiguities	• unwilling to "risk;" easily defeated by difficult words & text
• construct efficient strategies to monitor comprehension	• unable to construct efficient strategies to monitor comprehension
• stop to use a "fix-it" strategy when confused	• seldom use a "fix-it" strategy; plod on ahead, eager to finish
• reading skills improve	• reading progress is painfully slow

AFTER READING

Good Readers	Poor Readers
• understand how the pieces of information fit together	• do not understand how the pieces of information fit together
• able to identify what's salient	• may focus on the extraneous, peripheral
• interested in reading more	• see reading as distasteful

Adapted from The Orange County Public Schools, Department of Secondary Reading, Orlando Florida

Phase I:
BEFORE READING:
Giving Low Readers a "Head Start"

Rationale: General Class Discussions are Not Enough: Instead, Spark Their Interests by Activating Prior Knowledge and Focusing on the Purpose for Reading

Teacher-led explanations about the upcoming chapter are not enough to reach the reluctant learner who has a history of feeling incompetent in reading and disconnected from traditional class discussions. Students experiencing reading problems have experienced a loss of control over their ability to learn from textbooks; therefore, Phase I is the most critical phase for low readers. **Given the opportunity the day before to preview what they will be reading, they will be better prepared for the introduction of the lesson when it is presented in the content classroom**. Giving low readers a "head start" can be accomplished by asking open-ended questions formulated to accomplish three important objectives:

1) *to get students to think about what they already know about a topic,*

2) *to direct their focus and attention on a purpose for which they will be reading, and*

3) *to spark their interest and curiosity in the upcoming topic.*

The Power of Correct and Incorrect Prior Knowledge

What students comprehend, remember and infer from text has to do primarily with the "old" knowledge they are able to access. That in turn allows them to make sense of the "new" knowledge in the text. Their "old" knowledge can be **general** or highly **specific** about the upcoming topic. For example, a student may have **general** knowledge about *navigation* because of personal experiences with boats. When accessed, this "old knowledge" can make reading and thinking about Columbus's ocean voyages and his decisions about the routes he navigated far more meaningful.

> **Instruction therefore, must help readers *build upon and activate* their prior knowledge and make meaningful connections between what is familiar, what is known, what is experienced and what is about to be learned. Then attention is better focused on a reason to read, and reading becomes more gratifying because its purpose is now more apparent.**

One obvious way to begin the process of recognizing and valuing students' prior knowledge is to conduct informal and frequent inventories about their interests, strengths and meaningful experiences. When teachers deliberately capitalize on the unique interests and attributes of their students, reluctant learners can be wooed into participation in discussions, learning becomes more relevant, and discovering, constructing and reconstructing ideas are more likely to occur.

> **No matter what their reading capacity, all students have some knowledge that is pertinent, strengths, and interests that can be tapped. When teachers arm themselves with this powerful information to use when formulating pre-reading questions and discussions, they are recognizing the uniqueness of the individual student, and in doing so, helping him/her to feel good about learning, once again.**

During this Phase I, teachers can also determine how much a student knows and *does not know* about a topic. These discussions can offer both teachers and students the opportunity to identify strongly held myths and misconceptions that can also be used to build more meaningful bridges between old ways of thinking and new. **When teachers view misconceptions or gaps in knowledge as fruitful learning opportunities, reluctant learners begin to see that mistakes are not only "ok" but, in fact, useful and instructional.**

Activating students' prior knowledge and focusing their attention on the purpose for reading will *Give **Low Readers a***

Head Start. More specifically, they will be able to:

- think about what they already know about a subject;

- acquire a general understanding of how the BIG ideas will fit together

- understand the purpose for which they read; and therefore,

- **increase their confidence and motivation to read more.**

PHASE I SUGGESTIONS FOR LESSONS

Setting: Resource room, learning center, after school study tutorial or any other setting: PRIOR to the introduction of the lesson in the content classroom

Suggestion #1
Select Core Vocabulary

Introduce a carefully selected number of words and terms that appear in the selection. Textbook chapters contain a vast amount of information. Select "core" vocabulary by determining those words the student is likely to encounter again, or only those words germane to the main ideas of the lesson. Present words and terms on the board or on a simple form such as the one seen in the example below. Urge students to write an answer, if only a guess. Collect papers and return them to the students during Phase III or at the end of the lesson so they can fill in the last column and have the opportunity to review their initial responses. Initial "mistakes" should be viewed as instructional and used to help students become more aware of their own thinking and learning patterns.

Suggestion #2
Written Predictions

When students learn how to make reasonable predictions about what they will be reading, they are anticipating what

Figure 4-2a

Grade 5
CHAPTER 6
The First Colony, Jamestown

New chapter words/terms	What I think I already know	(to be completed in Phase III) What I *now* know

What is a *colony*?

Where was *Jamestown*?

What is a *stockholder*?

What is a *profit*?

What is an *indentured servant*?

What is *prosperity*?

What is a *plague*?

they think the author is going to say, and begin thinking about the purpose for which they read. **There are no right and wrong predictions. Therefore, students who have less confidence in their learning abilities can "feel" they can respond without risking yet another incorrect answer.**

Distribute triangle frames and emphasize that the base or bottom of the triangle is the largest area where students will be expected to do the most writing. Encourage students to write freely, creatively and phonetically (if they are unsure of how to spell a word). This an excellent activity for pairs or small groups of students. Collect the frames to redistribute during Phase III, when the chapter instruction is coming to an end.

Figure 4-2b

Grade 5
CHAPTER 6
The First Colony, Jamestown

New chapter words/terms	What I think I already know	(to be completed in Phase III) What I *now* know
What is a *colony?* **ANTS haVe coloNYs**		
Where was *Jamestown?* **?**		
What is a *stockholder?* **?**		
What is a *profit?* **MONEY MONEY**		
What is an *indentured servant?* **?**		
What is *prosperity?* **good times**		
What is a *plague?* **don't kNow**		

Suggestion #3
Use analogies and visual images in pre-reading discussions.

Analogies and visual images help students make meaningful links between what is familiar to them, what they know and what they are about to read. Analogies and visual images can be "fun" to think about because they help students construct "mental" pictures of ideas. They can also help students organize new information rendering it less arbitrary for easier retention and recall.

Analogies should be easy to learn and remember. Once students begin to exhibit analogous thinking, it should be

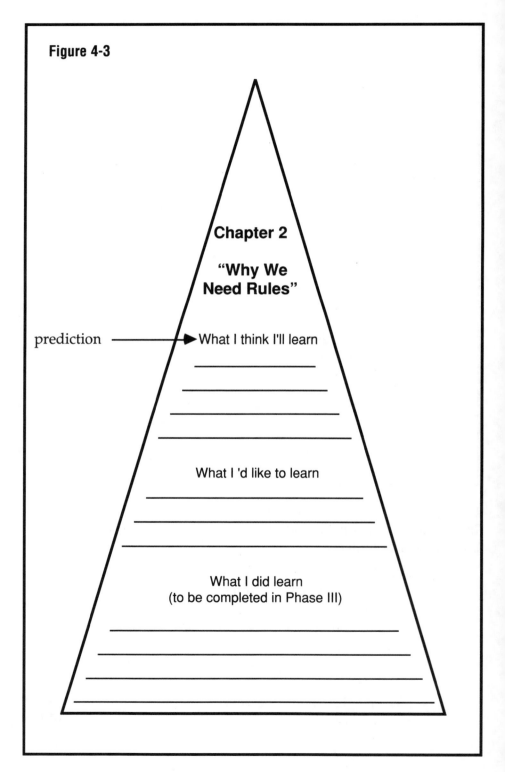

Figure 4-3

Chapter 2

"Why We
Need Rules"

prediction ——▶ What I think I'll learn

What I 'd like to learn

What I did learn
(to be completed in Phase III)

Figure 4-4

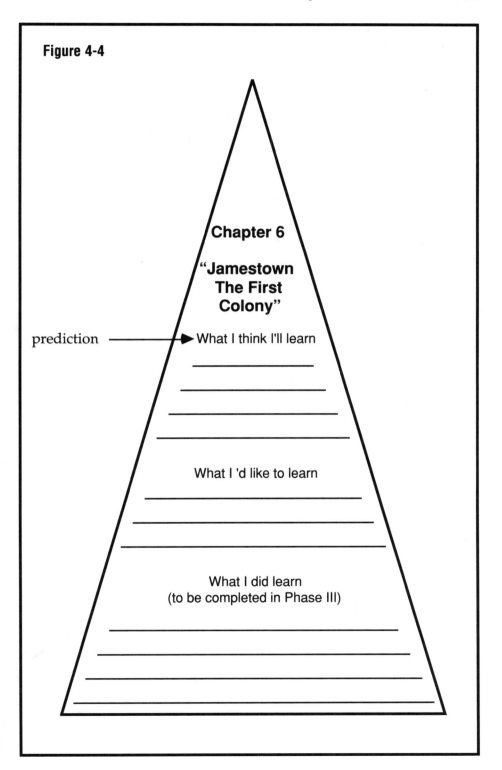

Chapter 6

"Jamestown
The First
Colony"

prediction ——▶ What I think I'll learn

What I 'd like to learn

What I did learn
(to be completed in Phase III)

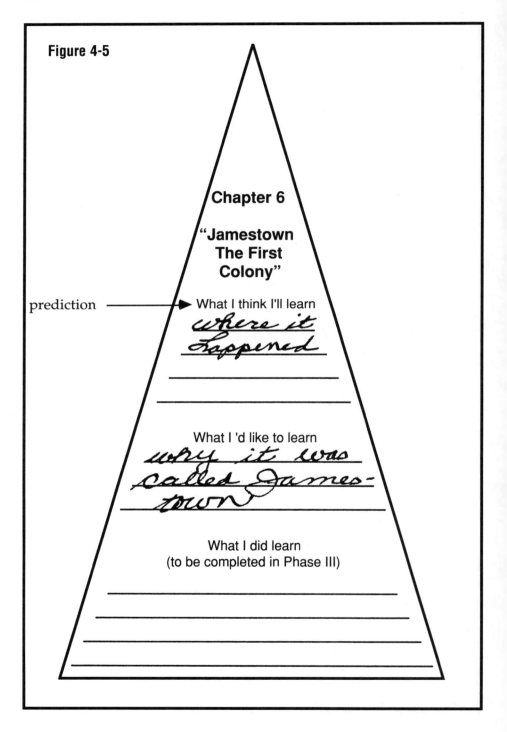

Figure 4-5

enthusiastically reinforced as it is a clear sign that in spite of low reading skills, they are developing their capacity to think abstractly.

Examples:

Analogies

to introduce new information..	*review familiar (old) information*
game of cricket	game of baseball
a school day in Japan	a school day in the U.S.
a tribe	a neighborhood

Suggestion 4
Distribute Concept Maps

Semantic maps or advanced organizers are simple, easy-to-read "maps" of words and terms presented to students **before, during and after** they read the textbook. When presented before reading, their purpose is to give students a *preview* of the important concepts and ideas in the textbook chapter and how they are related to one another.

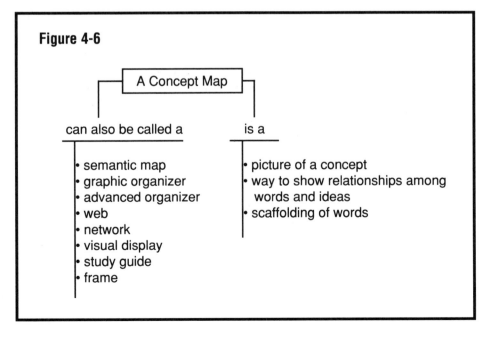

Figure 4-6

A Concept Map

can also be called a

- semantic map
- graphic organizer
- advanced organizer
- web
- network
- visual display
- study guide
- frame

is a

- picture of a concept
- way to show relationships among words and ideas
- scaffolding of words

Maps can differ depending upon whether they reflect a lesson that has flowed from the previously learned lesson, or if it is new information altogether. Basic guidelines to follow when designing maps include:

- If students already possess some conceptual knowledge about the upcoming lesson, less detailed, more general maps can be constructed.

- A map is effective when it conveys the relationships among ideas in a meaningful and explicit way rather than in arbitrary or implicit ways.

- A map is **not** effective when it is too specific, too literal, presents summaries or mere outlines.

Maps can also be powerful tools for collaborating teachers. Forced to clarify lesson goals in order to design the maps, instruction becomes more focused and illustrates yet another way of thinking about information. And maps and organizers are also excellent ways to communicate to parents. It offers them a *preview* of what their children will be expected to learn.

Distributed before the chapter is discussed, they serve to "prep" the students, giving them confidence to participate more fully in the upcoming textbook lesson. Maps can be partially complete, allowing the students to view the large structures of the new information but not all the important details. Later, as students read, they can add to the map's construction with new information.

All techniques described in Phase I can be accomplished in the resource room or learning center or any setting *prior* to the lesson beginning in the content classroom.

- conduct interest inventories
- tap prior knowledge
- make predictions
- use analogies and visual images
- distribute maps

Figure 4-7a

WORDS YOU WILL SEE IN THE CHAPTER ON EXPANSIONISM

(PEOPLE)———(IDEAS)———(PLACES)

PEOPLE	IDEAS	PLACES
Theodore Roosevelt		*Alaska*
Henry Cabot Lodge		
	The New Deal	
		Hawaii

Figure 4-7b

Minerals

SOFT MINERALS

Name	Hardness	Color	Function
Talc			used for powder
		grey	
	3	grey	
Fluorite	4		
		brown	

HARD MINERALS

Feldspar			
Quartz	7		used for radios
Topaz		blue	used for jewelry
Corundum	9		
		clear	used for jewelry

Scruggs, Mastropieri, Levin, McLoone, Gaffney & Prater, (1985).

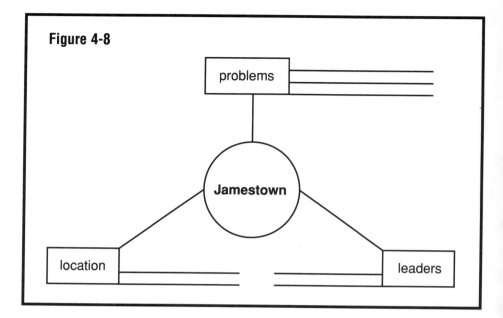

Figure 4-8

Most importantly, once the Phase I instructor selects and completes the techniques most appropriate, the student is ready to complete the Phase I process and make the transition to Phase II learning; that is, gathering the BIG ideas into a neat and manageable package that will equip him/her with the confidence, prior knowledge and interest in the lesson about to be presented in the content classroom! Armed with a preview of the new lesson, the student feels more in control, is more self-assured, more confident, and considerably more READY TO READ THE TEXTBOOK.

PHASE II: DURING READING: GETTING YOUR STUDENTS TO BECOME MORE ACTIVE COMPREHENDERS AND THINKERS

Rationale: Three reasons why lecture followed by oral or silent reading is not enough: helping your students become more active readers and thinkers.

Children and youth who have low reading skills often do not respond well to teacher-dominated, lengthy lectures and do not interact well with their textbooks during traditional oral or silent reading. When lectures are lengthy, the low reader feels little control over his/her own learning and becomes passive, losing track of what's been said; his attention fades.

When engaged in textbook reading, low readers tend to expend more time and energy struggling with individual words than on constructing meaning from the text. Unlike good readers who are more "automatic" in their ability to recognize familiar words and decode less familiar words, they often read slower, at the same rate of speed. This usually results in a slow, labored and choppy reading style that strains the reader's attention and interest, particularly during "sustained silent" reading that typifies homework assignments.

Secondly, as low readers overattend to individual words, they are less able to utilize the context to predict meaning. What results is a failure to activate or invent "self-help strategies," as they encounter ambiguous points in the textbook meaning. These strategies ordinarily include e.g., rereading the passage, more slowly, rehearsing a salient point, self-talking, jotting notes, etc.

Thirdly, as Chapter II (The Indomitable Textbook) discusses, matters are made clearly worse for the low reader because too many popular textbooks are organized so that main ideas are embedded, structures are implicit, and too many concepts are treated superficially. As these readers proceed to stumble on words, lose their place and concentration, they often lose the battle of understanding the meaning. They simply give up or refuse to read the textbook altogether. At this point, the important question becomes:

How do we teach low readers the strategies they need to suceed when the strategies can only be mastered while they are engaged in precisely the area they feel so lacking. . . reading.

Strategy Instruction

While the success of Phase I lies in the teacher's belief in the "power of prior knowledge," the success of Phase II is dependent upon the teachers' shift to more student-centered learning.

The teaching methodology referred to as "Strategy Instruction" requires that the content teacher relinquish the role of lecturer and instead learn and teach, specific instructional techniques that will draw the low reader into a more strategic and participatory role in the learning or reading activity.

Strategy instruction takes time to teach. It requires careful reflection on the teacher's part about **how to teach**: why, when and in what problems or circumstances to use a strategy. It involves frequent modeling and reteaching specific strategies when necessary.

The success of strategy instruction is heavily dependent upon on three criteria:

1) the commitment the teacher makes to acquire a repertoire of instructional strategies that have shown promise with low readers,

2) how well teachers can model their own strategic thinking, and

3) how well students are convinced that strategies are useful in improving their grades.

Experts in the field of strategy instruction (Pressley, 1990; Swanson, 1989; Wong, 1985), have made the following useful observations about teachers and strategy teaching.

Strategies take time to learn. For a student with a history of learning problems, it may take many years for them to become proficient at using a particular strategy in an appropriate problem application without prompting. Students need sustained high-quality strategy instruction in order to:

1) become better at paying attention to what's important in the text,

Figure 4-9

Good Strategy Teachers	Not So Good Strategy Teachers
make sure that strategy instruction is well planned and continuous	provide fragmented, "hit or miss" strategy instruction
overtly "model" covert self-regulation thoughts; *for example:* ["In class today... we're going to do 3 things. The **first thing we're going to** do is. .. The second thing we're going to do is... and the **third** thing we're going to do is...]	tend to be unaware of own mental processes
identify and teach strategy prerequisites before teaching strategy; *for example:* ["Before we open our books to learn how to preview text structures, let's make sure we all remember the 3 most common structures found history books. If you think you might forget these structures later, what should you do now?"]	tend to ignore prerequisite or teach them and the strategy at the same time
focus strategy instruction of what we are doing and why *for example:* ["Remember, we're looking for text structures so we can improve our chances of remembering the important ideas here and therefore do better on the chapter test next week. Look back on the 6 pages read yesterday. What did you decide were the common structures?"]	focus strategy instruction on memorization of strategy steps
work hard to get students to self-regulate, set their own goals and self-reinforce	set goals for students/exaggerate praise/use extrinsic reinforcers
know that strategy learning takes time and effort *for example:* ["It may be several weeks before you'll be able to recognize the structures in your textbook. Give yourself time. It takes practice."]	expect students to benefit immediately

Adapted from: Ellis, Deshler, Lenz, Schumaker & Clark, 1991

✗2) become more aware of their points of confusion, and

✗3) better at organizing and remembering what they read.

Ideally, strategy practice should take place in small cooperative learning groups and involve a variety of reading materials such as trade books, newspapers and the textbook.

A major caution: often students with learning problems may learn to verbalize how to do the strategy, but fail to understand when and how to use it without prompting. Continued dialogue and support for particular individuals as they strive to use the strategies are vital to be sure each student is using the strategy effectively.

Not all strategies are appropriate for all low readers and for all reading tasks, and not all strategies have been scientifically validated. However—teachers can discover the reading and thinking strategies that work best over time in order to help students in their ability to:

- better attend to words and meaning simultaneously
- cope more effectively with text ambiguities
- develop self help comprehension and study strategies; and therefore,
- **be motivated to read more.**

PHASE II SUGGESTIONS FOR LESSONS

Setting: Content Classroom

Suggestion #1
Reciprocal Teaching Techniques.

Reciprocal teaching techniques (Palinscar & Brown, 1986), are particularly effective in helping low readers acquire a sense of control over their learning because students assume more dominant roles in the learning process. This is achieved by teaching students how to lead discussions about the text. In reciprocal teaching, teachers and students are partners in jointly constructing the meaning of the text through four processes that require initial teacher modelling and then less teacher and more student involvement. And as opportunities occur for more students to participate, the diversity among their cultural and linguistic background, prior knowledge, experiences, unique strengths and interests can be more effectively utilized. Executed carefully, the steps in reciprocal teaching can build upon Phase I learning. With careful planning, the method takes approximately ten days for the teacher and students to master:

Step 1

Set aside one entire class period to learn about four ideas that form the underpinnings of reciprocal teaching: *questions* (why they are important and how to phrase them); *predictions* (what are they, why they are important and how to phrase them); *summaries* (what are they, why they are important and when are they useful); *clarifications* (what are they, why are they important, and how to phrase them). Review this discussion regularly as needed.

Step 2

Assign reading for 10 to 20 minutes.

Step 3

"Model" by orally summarizing the reading assignment: Reformulate the main ideas, important details, text structures and emerging patterns.

Then "model" self-questioning: **Ask**: *What was the problem? the solution? the cause? the effect? The order of events?*

Then clarify ambiguities. **Ask**, *What did the author mean when she said. . . what does the word on page x mean?*

Then predict the upcoming section; *what will the author say next about the. . . ? What's going to happen when. . . ?*

After teacher modelling of the four processes, students take turns leading the dialogues. As students speak, teachers can draw maps or webs of the constructed and reconstructed text. Students are then assigned the next lesson to read and the processes continue. Over time, students become more adept at leading dialogues and comprehending, at a deeper level, the meaning of their textbook lessons. (see: Palinscar & Brown, 1986: "Interactive teaching to promote independent learning from text.")

Suggestion #2

(INSERT)

INSERT was developed by Vaughn and Estes (1986), as an active reading technique. It is a particularly useful way for low readers to become more aware of **a breakdown in comprehension** so that they can remember to clarify the ambiguity at a later point in time. This is a particularly useful strategy when students own their own books and are free to mark them. But if marking or photocopying the reading assignment is a problem, students can use "post-it" notes or strips of paper in the margin of the text.

Assign students pages to read for homework or class work by first reviewing the following scheme. Ask students to copy the symbols on a sturdy blank book marker to use while they are engaged in the reading activity.

Marking system for INSERT

X	I thought differently
+	New information
!	WOW
??	I don't understand
*	Very important

Students can also be encouraged to "invent" their own codes or symbols. In doing so, they will think about the way they think, and move more steadily toward independent learning.

Suggestion #3
Mapping Strategies

Prepare reading maps or teach students **how** to construct their own. Reading maps can be extensions of concept maps (introduced in Phase I), or newly constructed maps for reading. Maps can be particularly effective during Phase II because they can help readers focus on what is salient in the text, as well as help them monitor their comprehension. **And because reading maps can combine visual or graphic symbols with words and phrases, they tend to be a more appealing task than traditional note taking or outlining.**

As in reciprocal teaching, teachers should **model** on a regular basis, how to construct reading maps by using an overhead projector or the board. Teachers must also speak clearly about their reasons behind each part of the map-construction. Gradually students should be able to independently construct their own.

Examples of reading maps:
Distribute the following map immediately prior to the reading assignment explaining to students to fill in the missing information as they read:

Construct reading maps that will teach readers to think about TEXT STRUCTURES. Readers should be encouraged to construct additions, pictures or any other "cue" that will help them organize and remember the text. Distribute maps such as those below for students to use while reading.

Suggestion #4
Teach students how to take short summary notes.

Summary notes are often difficult because they require students to condense information by focusing on what's salient and ignoring what's extraneous. Good summary notes highlight the main idea(s), include only important details and

Figure 4-10

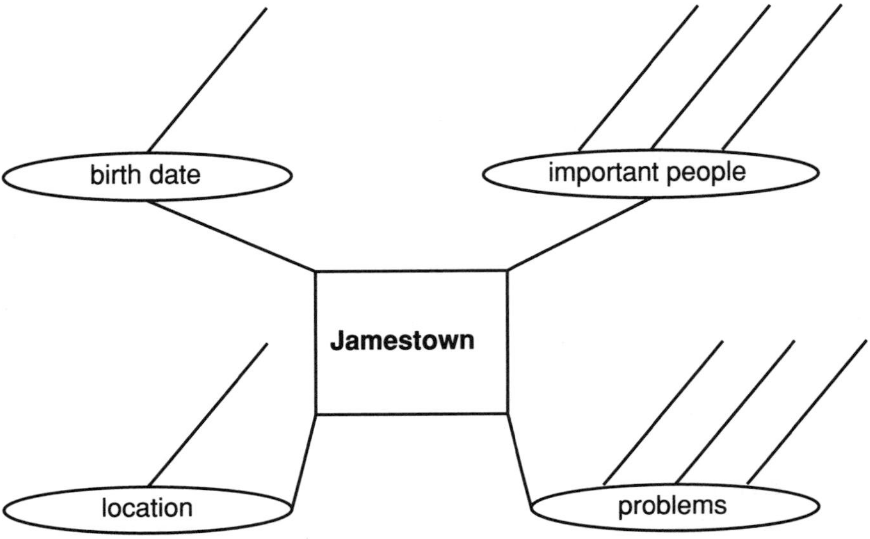

birth date

important people

Jamestown

location

problems

Figure 4-11
Indian Tribes

	Northeast	Southwest	Plains
Clothing			
Food			
Shelter			
Travel			

Gaskins & Elliot, 1991, p. 72

Figure 4-12

PROBLEMS faced by the colonists   SOLUTIONS

1. _____   _____

2. _____   _____

3. _____   _____

4. _____   _____

5. _____   _____

Figure 4-13

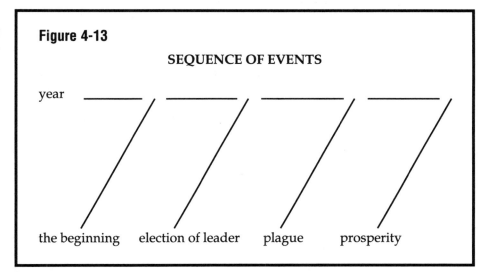

SEQUENCE OF EVENTS

year

the beginning   election of leader   plague   prosperity

Figure 4-14

(3) CAUSES of the plague   (2) EFFECTS of the plague

1. _____   1. _____

2. _____   2. _____

3. _____   3. _____

4. _____

convey a correct sequence of events. The following are simple steps to teach students the summary note strategy:

- assign students the reading task
- segment the assignment into 4 – 8 "chunks" and ask students to note each segment and make one summary note for each "chunk"
- instruct students to first construct one map per "chunk" of assigned text by writing the title of the passage in the center of the map, place 2-4 main ideas in a circle around the title and write 1-3 important details under each main idea.
- then ask students to use their maps to help them write short summaries for each "chunk" of text.

Once students have finished the reading and summary note exercise, they can collaborate in small groups, exchange papers offering a useful window into one another's way of thinking. At that point there is an opportunity to readjust, refine or otherwise improve upon their summary notes.

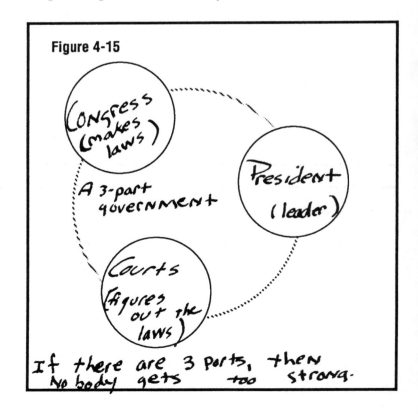

Figure 4-15

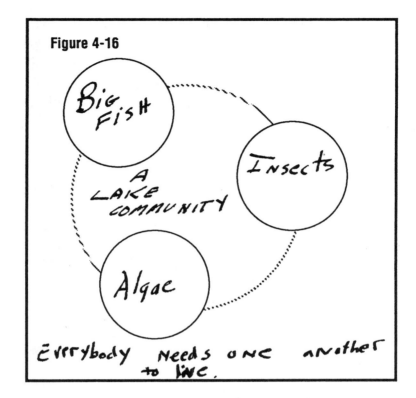

Figure 4-16

Big Fish

A LAKE COMMUNITY

Insects

Algae

Everybody Needs one another to live.

Suggestion #5
Transactional Strategy Instruction

Transactional strategy instruction emphasizes a coordinated use of a variety of strategies through direct explanations and modeling (see: Pressley, El-Dinary, Gaskins, Schuder, Bergman, Almari, & Brown, 1992 for a complete review of transactional instruction). This method requires teachers to pay as much attention to helping students understand **the thinking behind their responses and strategy use** as to the teaching of the strategies per se. The goals of transactional strategy instruction include not only improving academic performance through strategy use, but strengthening students' commitments to learning. More specifically, transactional strategy instruction involves:

- teachers and students **jointly** constructing and reconstructing meaning from the text;

- offering students a small number of strategies during any given lesson and demonstrating how to use and coordinate them with previously learned strategies;

- frequent discussions about the "natural" use of strategies and how they are related to the textbook content;

- building motivation and a commitment to reading.

Example:
Mrs. Romaine begins her fifth grade social studies class by discussing what reading strategies her students like best and why. (e.g., thinking aloud, rereading, mapping, imaging the text, discovering an analogy, jotting down short summaries, mapping the text, using INSERT, predicting, paraphrasing, etc.). She reviews with them:

- the nature of the strategy (s);

- why they are valuable, and

- surveys her student's ideas about the best time to use them.

Together Mrs. Romaine and her students make the relationship between the strategy and the content explicit as she models her own strategic thinking and reading behavior by reading a short text aloud to the class.

At the same time, Mrs. Romaine is sensitive to each individual student's responses to the task, particularly how efficient and flexible her students become in strategy use. She emphasizes the connections between *old knowledge* and *new knowledge* and works hard over time to get her students to make these connections without her.

PHASE III: AFTER READING: GETTING STUDENTS TO CONSOLIDATE AND EXTEND THEIR TEXTBOOK KNOWLEDGE

Rationale: Traditional questions and paper and pencil tests are not sufficient ways to help students retain new knowledge. Instead, help students keep track of their progress and extend what they learn in their textbook to their personal world.

While part of the success in Phases I and II lies in the teacher's belief in the power of the students' prior knowledge, and a commitment to student-centered learning, the success of Phase III has much to do with the teacher's ability to guide students in learning to connect and consolidate the new knowledge from previous learning and experiences both in and out of the classroom.

Phase III strategies will help students:

- understand how the pieces of the information fit together;
- learn how to identify what is salient, what is extraneous;
- interest them in reading more.

Phase III Suggested Lessons

Setting: Content classroom or resource room, learning center, after school tutorial

Suggestion #1. *Complete vocabulary/prediction forms from Phase I*

Redistribute vocabulary or written prediction forms from Phase I and have students complete the third column. Most importantly, have students study their own shifts in thinking by comparing their responses in column 1 to those in column 2.

Suggestion #2. *Have students analyze end-of-the-chapter questions*

Students enjoy this activity because it does not require that they answer questions. Rather it helps them to learn about ways to use questions to think about the content. Teach students how to discriminate among three types of end-of-the-chapter questions:

1) questions looking for literal or factual answers,

2) questions that ask students to make inferences or analyses, and

3) questions asking students for their opinions.

Figure 4-17

Grade 5
CHAPTER 6
The First Colony, Jamestown

New chapter words/terms	What I think I already know	(to be completed in Phase III) What I *now* know
What is a *colony*?		
Where was *Jamestown*?		
What is a *stockholder*?		
What is a *profit*?		
What is an *indentured servant*?		
What is *prosperity*?		
What is a *plague*?		

When students learn how to discriminate among the three types of questions, they can learn how to formulate their own questions when reading. They can also learn they can save time by not looking for the answer in the textbook to an "opinion" question.

Suggestion #3 *Have students extend their concept maps.*

Once again, mapping is an effective way to consolidate learning once the text has been read, and can also be an alternative to testing. For those students who have found reading to be distasteful, mapping exercises can serve as an incentive to

Figure 4-18

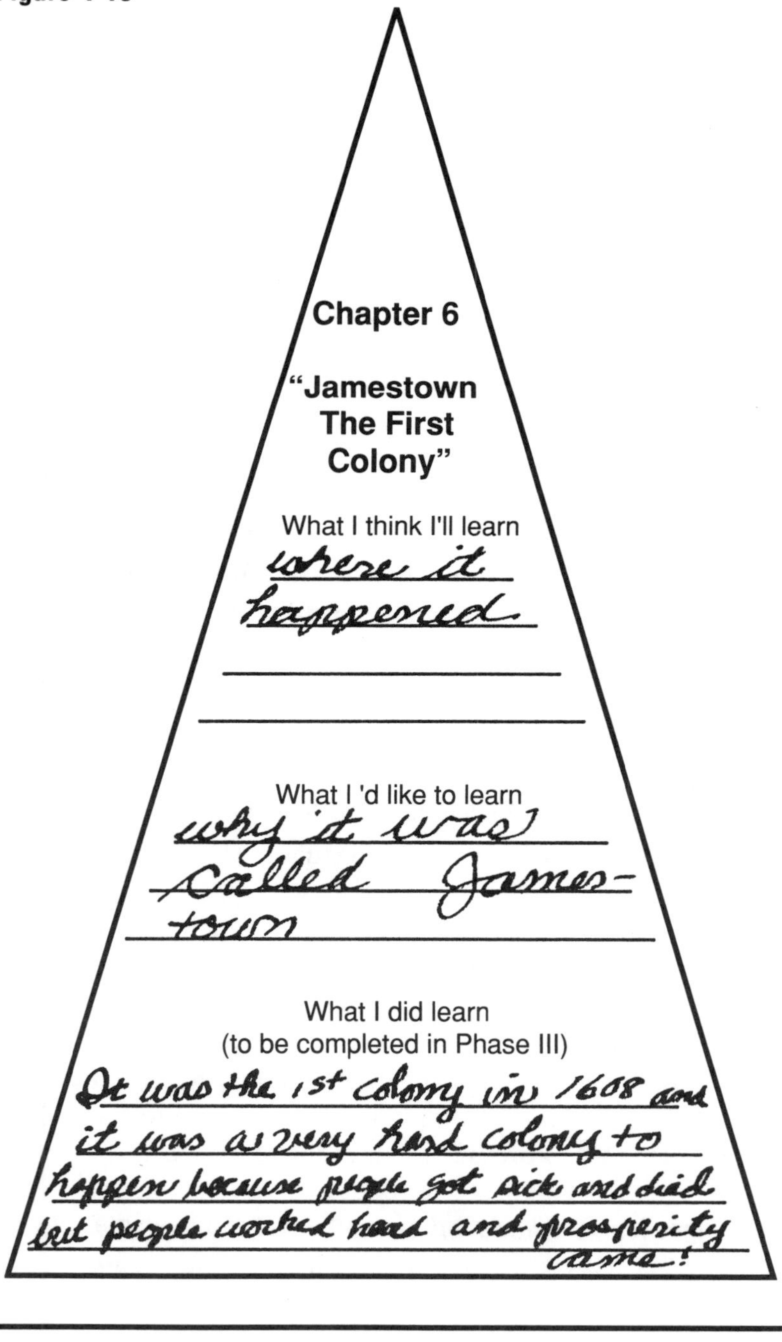

Chapter 6

**"Jamestown
The First
Colony"**

What I think I'll learn

*where it
happened.*

What I 'd like to learn

*why it was
called James-
town*

What I did learn
(to be completed in Phase III)

*It was the 1st colony in 1608 and
it was a very hard colony to
happen because people got sick and died
but people worked hard and prosperity
came!*

reread. Moreover, by Phase III, mapping should be a familiar task, as practice and repetition produce feelings of success and confidence. Low readers can begin to discover ways to become better at mapping, improving and creating new maps as they proceed through the textbook chapters.

- Students can add-on from previous maps or make new ones.

- Gradually they can experiment with more symbols, pictures, colors, words or phrases.

- Students can work collaboratively in study groups or independently.

The idea is for students to use words and visual cues to make connections among ideas in the textbooks. In this way, theybegin to process information at a deeper and more meaningful level that should subsequently facilitate retention and recall.

But even more importantly, students should spend time discussing their reasons behind their map-construction decisions. This process can not only enhance classroom interactions but can influence motivation to read and reading competence.

Suggestion #4 *Have students go back and look for text structures.*

Initially, the structures could be made explicit on a frame such as:

Then over time, distribute frames which contain less information that force the reader to become more independent at discriminating among structures.

When students are able to independently identify text structures, they will not only improve in their ability to remember important information but they will also improve in their ability to organize and express their thoughts on paper.

Suggestion #5 *Show good examples and bad examples of writing.*

Students who are low readers benefit more from practice in reading and writing of extended text rather than from filling in one word answers to end-of-the-lesson questions. But all too often, low readers read without making distinctions between the main

Figure 4-19

Causes of Volcanoes	→	**Effects** of Volcanoes

_____   _____

_____   _____

_____   _____

_____   _____

_____   _____

_____   _____

Figure 4-20

TOPIC: _____

Causes	→	Effects

_____   _____

_____   _____

OR

Problem	→	Solution

_____   _____

_____   _____

Figure 4-21   The Sequence of Events

year

event   •   •   •   •

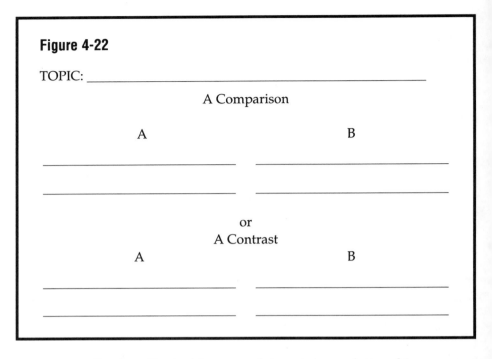

Figure 4-22

TOPIC: _____

A Comparison

A   B

_____   _____

_____   _____

or
A Contrast

A   B

_____   _____

_____   _____

and subordinate ideas, or determining relationships among ideas. As a result, their written summaries are often a mixed "grocery list" of ideas and details, without evident organization.

Nonetheless, students can learn how to summarize especially if the BIG ideas became apparent to them before reading, (Phase I) and subsequently reinforced through an active (during) reading process (Phase II). Written summaries are excellent ways for students to demonstrate comprehension and novel thinking.

Prepare two written models that summarize the text and place them on the overhead next to one another. Work toward getting students to see the differences between the two written summaries. One "summary" should be a "grocery list" of separate details. The other should:

1. place the main idea clearly up front

2. chunk similar information

3. omit minor details

4. reflect author's position

5. be the correct length (approximately one-third of text).

Distribute lined paper with the above criteria written in bold letters at the top of the page. Have students work in small groups where they can summarize the text, exchange and edit one another's summaries.

Suggestion #6 *Distribute Frames for Identifying Problem/Solutions or Causes and Effects*

Suggestion #7 *Reinforce voluntary recreational reading of topics that relate to the textbook chapter.*

Recreational reading is not only a powerful source of growth in vocabulary, spelling and writing but can also help students make gains on standardized reading tests.

Trade books or magazines should be:

- readily available in the class,
- self-selected by the reader,
- available on the reader's *independent* reading level.

Figure 4-23

The biggest problem in Chapter 7 was _____
_____

It started when _____
_____

After that _____
_____

Then _____
_____

The problem was solved when _____
_____

The chapter made me think about_____
_____

Good teachers can maximize the use of even a mediocre textbook, particularly if they love to teach, are excited about their subject area, are willing to collaborate with the student's remedial teachers or tutors, and enjoy making learning fun. In a climate of increasing student diversity, teachers who possess the ability to foster trust between themselves and their students may be the teachers who are ultimately the most successful. Trust between the teacher and the student who has experienced considerable academic failures and frustrations can be the beginning of self-determination for the student, a willingness to take risks and ultimately the confidence to want to learn more (Ensminger & Dangel, 1992).

An Effective Teacher of Content:
Is a lover of content
Is a strategic thinker
Can collaborate if necessary

---

and. . .

- spends time thinking about ways to capitalize on her/his students' strengths and helping students make connections between their experiences and learning textbook content;

- feels that HOW one learns is as important as WHAT one learns;

- has high expectations for all students, especially low readers, and challenges students of all ability levels;

- teaches reading, thinking and content concurrently;

- is a strategy teacher who models his/her own strategy thinking "out loud" or in other observable ways;

- works closely with the resource room or remedial teacher and sets up paired reading structures, peer tutoring, after school study sessions, or other cooperative learning structures in or out of the content classroom. See figure 4-24 for a contrast in the approaches for teaching low readers we've been discussing.

Figure 4-24
A Shift in the Way to Teach Low Readers in the Content Classroom

	Old Way	*New Way*
Before Reading	Teacher provides a brief discussion of the new chapter	Teachers regard this as a critical phase of instruction; (e.g., pre-reading activities may take place in the resource room **prior** to the introduction of the chapter in the content classroom).
During Reading	Assigns pages to read and end of the lesson questions to write for homework, and asks students to be prepared to discuss text lectures, discusses and asks questions.	Assigns part of reading and writing in class so that guided reading and other strategies can be practiced; connections to material are frequently made explicit.
After Reading	Written tests	Students collaborate and study with one another to prepare for tests. Novel Projects such as chapter maps that demonstrate comprehension are encouraged; the transition to the next chapter begins.

A Student Who Uses Textbooks Well:

- learns how to think about his/her prior knowledge when reading "new" ideas in their textbooks;

- learns how to better monitor his/her comprehension (and confusion);

- gradually develops a repertoire of reading, thinking and study strategies and masters the ones that work best;

- becomes confident enough to create and test his/her own strategies;

- is able to make connections with what s/he learns from books to his/her personal world and community.

Note: For a detailed account of strategy instruction research, see Pressley and Associates, (1990) *Cognitive Strategy Instruction That Really Improves Academic Performance,* Cambridge, MA.: Brookline Books.

CHAPTER 5

What Does
A Really Good Textbook
Look Like?

Textbook selection committee members are rarely allocated the time and support necessary to actually read the textbook to assess its quality in terms of content and instructional characteristics. Instead, topic and readability checklists, and copyright dates remain the major determinants for selecting textbooks. Most importantly, little guidance is available to help teachers estimate the text difficulty so that they can determine if the text is a suitable match for their students (Chall and Conard, 1991).

A second major barrier to improving the textbook selection process is that all too often, special educators do not participate in textbook adoptions, nor do they have the perception that they should. Teachers who **do** participate are rarely trained in looking for specific features in textbooks that can improve its utility with the growing population of low readers in the general education content classroom (Fiore, Danin, Nero, 1992).

Teachers, in general, and special and remedial educators must acquire knowledge about the relationships between learner and text characteristics, so they can participate fully in text selection decisions. They must also be *given the time and support to read the book* in order to assess its organization and cohesion across lessons, chapters and units.

To assist you in sharpening your textbook consumer skills, review the following guidelines. They can help you in what can often be a complex decision-making process.

The following textbook analysis maps may also be helpful in the process of comparing and contrasting textbook programs. Reconstruct the map to match your particular needs or

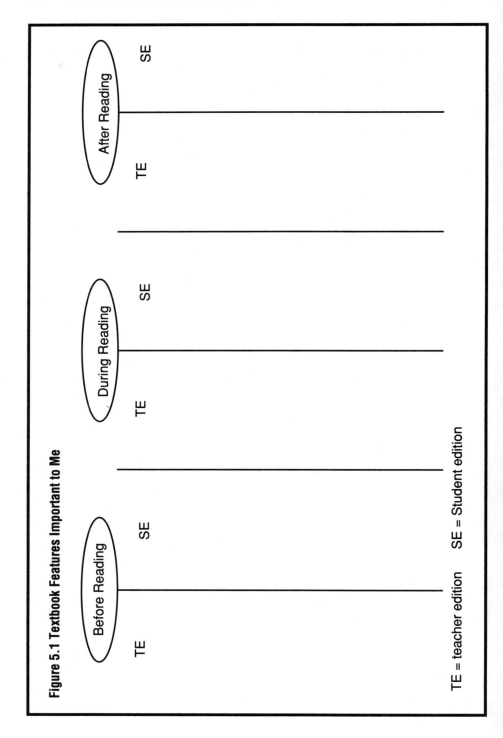

Figure 5.1 Textbook Features Important to Me

invent any other evaluation strategy that works best for you and your colleagues.

Broad guidelines to follow when looking for good textbooks to use in classrooms with a wide range of reading abilities:

1. Choose textbook programs that clearly reflect the importance of the three phases of teaching and learning, particularly programs that pay serious attention to the *pre*-reading stage.

2. Look for textbooks that contain questions and activities that reinforce the links among higher order thinking skills, reading and writing skills.

3. Look for textbooks that are examples of good and lively writing rather than textbooks that are written to conform to a readability level.

4. Look for textbooks that contain exciting graphics and illustrations that magnify and complement the text, not replace it.

5. Look for textbooks that include activities that help students make meaningful connections with their community and home interests.

6. Look for textbooks that either guide the teacher about how to construct concept maps (i.e., semantic map, graphic organizer, advanced organizer, web, network, visual display, study guide, frame) or provide samples of maps in the ancillary materials.

The reader should feel free to copy pages 70-79 for evaluating textbooks for your personal use or your textbook committee's use.

Figure 5-2
Specific Guidelines to Follow When Looking for
Good Textbooks for Students with Low Reading Skills

E= excellent
G= good
P= poor

Part I: Before Reading   **NAMES OF TEXTBOOKS**

1. New knowledge should build upon and explicitly relate to previously learned skills and knowledge. Look for guidance at the beginning of chapter or units about prerequisite knowledge and skills, and the location of this information in the textbook.

Example:

This chapter [on the Pilgrims] requires general background knowledge about:

1) Native American Indians (see pp. xx)

2) European exploration (see pp.xx) and specific knowledge about the concepts of:

3) expeditions

4) settlements

5) commissions

RATINGS

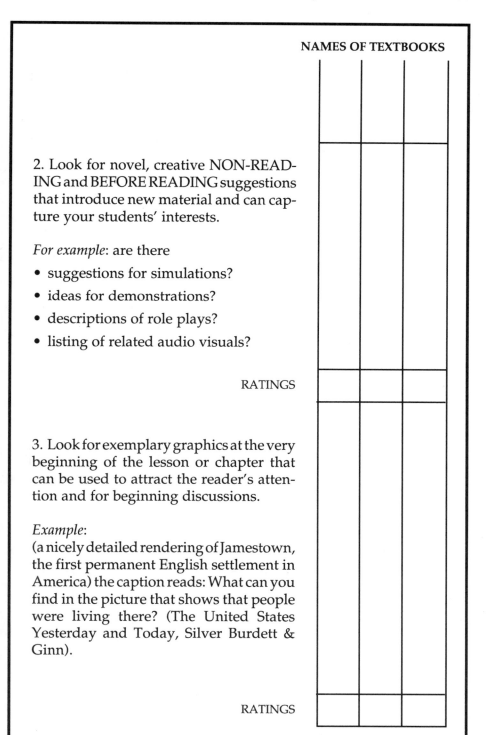

NAMES OF TEXTBOOKS

2. Look for novel, creative NON-READING and BEFORE READING suggestions that introduce new material and can capture your students' interests.

For example: are there

- suggestions for simulations?
- ideas for demonstrations?
- descriptions of role plays?
- listing of related audio visuals?

RATINGS

3. Look for exemplary graphics at the very beginning of the lesson or chapter that can be used to attract the reader's attention and for beginning discussions.

Example:
(a nicely detailed rendering of Jamestown, the first permanent English settlement in America) the caption reads: What can you find in the picture that shows that people were living there? (The United States Yesterday and Today, Silver Burdett & Ginn).

RATINGS

NAMES OF TEXTBOOKS

4. Look for ways the textbook pays attention to activating prior knowledge, particularly books on the secondary level.

For example:

- Are there discussions of the importance of prior knowledge in the teacher materials?
- Are there oral or written exercises that help students activate prior knowledge?
- Is there use of the pronoun "you" in the text or in captions that serves to activate a reader's prior knowledge (e.g., "have you ever seen a tumbleweed?")

RATINGS

5. Look for short but well-written preview statements.

For example:

- [preview statement] In this chapter, you will read about what the Pilgrims were looking for when they landed at Plymouth, Massachusetts and what happened to them after they arrived.

RATINGS

NAMES OF TEXTBOOKS

6. Look for short but well-written summary statements that relate well to the preview statement.

For example:

• This chapter was about the Pilgrims' search for a better way of life in America and the experiences they had when they moved to a new land and met new and different people.

RATINGS

7. Given the likelihood that all chapters will not be covered in a school year, look for books that provide guidance about making informed choices about how to select which chapters, units, concepts and vocabulary words to teach.

For example:

• Is the core information or major themes designated or marked?
• Is there helpful information in deciding what to teach;
• Is the vocabulary that students are likely to encounter later on in the text marked?

RATINGS

NAMES OF TEXTBOOKS

8. Look at titles and subtitles and determine if they reflect an accurate and logical flow of the content.

Look for correspondence between the title and text structure.

Look to see if titles and subtitles contain useful information for the reader who may be previewing the text.

For Example:
Poor Heading   *Improved Heading*

[chapter title]
The Lay   The Climate &
of the Land   Geography of Louisiana
(ambiguous structure)   (descriptive structure)

[chapter subtitles]
From Marsh   Louisiana has Both Marshes
to Mountain   & Mountains
(vague description)   (tells reader more clearly they
                             will be reading about
                             extremes in the topography)

In Ancient Times   How the Land Called
                            Louisiana was Formed in
                            Ancient Times
(ambiguous structure)   (sets up a chronology
                             structure)

The Father   The Mighty Mississippi and
& His Children   Other Rivers
(nonexistent structure)   (descriptive structure)

RATINGS

NAMES OF TEXTBOOKS

9. Look in the ancillary materials for concept maps or other taxonomies that coincide with the introduction of vocabulary, help students make connections to previously learned material and prior knowledge, *or* guidance about how to construct them.

For example:

[chapter on the arrival of the Pilgrims at Plymouth]
    DIFFERENCES IN THE WAY PEOPLE LIVE

Native Americans The Pilgrims   Me
[old lesson]   [new lesson]   [prior experience]

                  favorite food

_____   _____   _____

                  shelter/home

_____   _____   _____

                  3 wishes

_____   _____   _____

RATINGS

10. Look for books that identify which lessons, chapter or units lend themselves well to mapping exercises in the event teachers and students want to construct their own.

RATINGS

NAMES OF TEXTBOOKS

Part II. During Reading

1. Look for "considerate" textbooks that contain structural features that can enhance reading comprehension and thinking.

For example:
Are the paragraphs deductively organized so that main ideas are explicit or stated up front, rather than inductively organized and main ideas are implicit or inferred?

Inductively organized paragraph
Arkansas was a territory of the United States from 1819 until 1836. * **During that time, she was governed by an interesting group of leaders.** They often fought and killed each other. In the main they were an able group of men. They met and solved many important problems. They located a new capital and built a statehouse. Under them the territory grew in population and wealth preparing for the day when it would become a state (p.83 "Our Arkansas" Steck-Vaughn).

*main idea is embedded

NAMES OF TEXTBOOKS

Deductively organized paragraph
* Arkansas was governed by a group of interesting men while she was still a territory of the United States. They often fought and killed each other. In the main they were an able group of men. They met and solved many important problems. They located a new capital and built a statehouse. From 1819, the territory grew in population and wealth preparing for the day it would become a state in 1836.

*main idea is stated up front

For example:

• Are the connectives and referents clear, and are the pictures, illustrations and other graphics clearly related to the message in the text (rather than exist in place of the text)?

• Is there useful information in the titles and subtitles?

• Are the books enjoyable to read? Are the chapters written in an engaging and consistent writing style rather than dull, contrived text and/or chapters written in very different genres.

RATINGS

NAMES OF TEXTBOOKS

2. Look for books that discuss the importance of weaving reading and thinking strategies into the teaching of content and provide information on when, how and why to use various strategies.

RATINGS

3. Look for books that discuss the importance of cooperative learning and highlight the lessons, chapters and units that lend themselves well to cooperative learning structures.

RATINGS

Part III: After Reading

1. Look for books that pay serious attention to teaching higher order thinking skills and writing of extended text.

For example:

- Do the end of the lesson, chapter or unit questions require writing of extended text rather than factual questions that require one-word answers?

- Do assessments and other activities reinforce the connections between reading, thinking and writing?

RATINGS

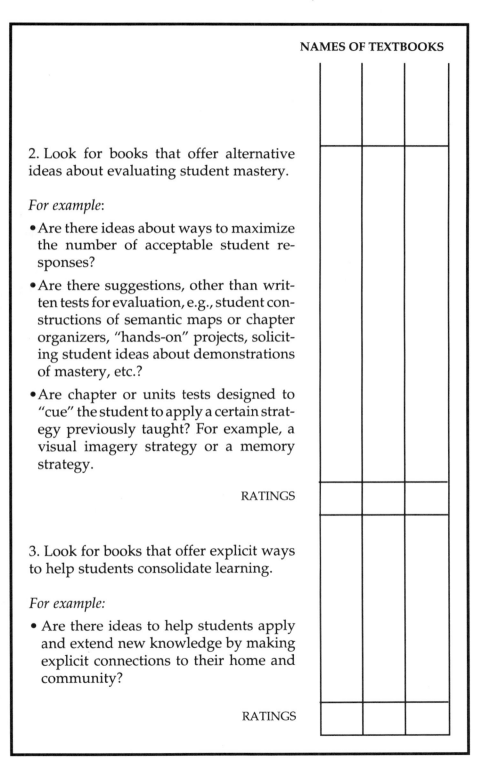

NAMES OF TEXTBOOKS

2. Look for books that offer alternative ideas about evaluating student mastery.

For example:

• Are there ideas about ways to maximize the number of acceptable student responses?

• Are there suggestions, other than written tests for evaluation, e.g., student constructions of semantic maps or chapter organizers, "hands-on" projects, soliciting student ideas about demonstrations of mastery, etc.?

• Are chapter or units tests designed to "cue" the student to apply a certain strategy previously taught? For example, a visual imagery strategy or a memory strategy.

RATINGS

3. Look for books that offer explicit ways to help students consolidate learning.

For example:

• Are there ideas to help students apply and extend new knowledge by making explicit connections to their home and community?

RATINGS

CONCLUSION

Although educational publishers have begun to pay attention to the needs of a more "diverse" student body, (Ciborowski, Antes, Zorfass & Ames, 1989), it is an extremely difficult task for them to accomplish. On the one hand, average and above average readers possess the skills that allow them to more readily "grapple" with text ambiguities. In the process of this struggle, they become better readers. On the other hand, students who have reading problems haven't the necessary resources for the struggle and are easily overwhelmed. But both groups need textbooks that are suitably challenging, yet manageable.

Fortunately, teachers not textbooks teach students (Flood, 1986). So while researchers continue to work to reach a better understanding of the most desirable match between the books and the students who use them, practitioners must discover ways to woo the reluctant learner back to the content classroom and make learning feel good again.

The Study: Improving Textbook Usability Final Report

ABSTRACT

In 1985, with funding from the U.S. Department of Education, Office of Special Education, Education Development Center (EDC) in Newton Massachusetts, and RMC Research Corporation in Hampton, New Hampshire, undertook a project to improve textbooks for students experiencing learning problems. The project involved a qualitative analysis of 12 widely used social studies and science textbook programs and culminated in a national conference for teachers, publishers and researchers in Washington, D.C.

Because so many learning and reading disabled student are "mainstreamed" for social studies, history, and science classes, and spend more than half their instructional time engaged in textbook learning, three initial goals were pursued:

1) a determination of common learner characteristics;

2) the identification of effective instructional strategies that have shown promise with learning and reading disabled students;

3) a determination of textbook features known to facilitate or hinder comprehension and recall.

Textbook analysis findings revealed a generally poor to adequate quality of the instructional design of content textbook programs. As a result, they make the task of getting information unduly difficult for students, particularly students with poor reading skills. Moreover, when textbooks try to treat too many concepts in too little depth, when main ideas and structures are not made explicit and when writing is dull, matters are made clearly worse for the reading disabled student. Recommendations clustered around three major themes:

1) guidelines for publishers to design better written textbooks,

2) an instructional model for teachers to use with existing textbooks, and

3) a textbook analysis tool which can help practitioners identify well designed as well as poorly designed textbooks.

ANALYZING THE TWELVE TEXTBOOK PROGRAMS

How Were Textbooks Selected?

In order to determine the most "widely used" social studies and science textbook programs, a variety of organizations were contacted for information regarding publishers' market standings in elementary and secondary textbook sales. These organizations included the Association of American Publishers, the International Reading Association, Market Data Retrieval, The Educational Products Information Exchange, textbook adoption researchers, textbook monitoring groups, science and social studies curriculum centers, members of major textbook adoption committees, professional organizations in science and social studies education, and a variety of educational publishers. Each source was asked to identify publishers believed to hold the largest share of the market in each subject area and grade level.

Three copies of the teacher and pupil editions of each textbook program identified were subsequently acquired for use in the upcoming appraisal.

Textbooks Analyzed

SCIENCE

Science, Silver Burdett (1987) Grade 1

Heath Science, D.C. Heath (1985) Grade 3

Holt Science, Holt, Rinehart, & Winston (1986), Grade 5

SOCIAL STUDIES

Families & Neighborhoods Silver Burdett (1986), Grade 1

City, Town & Country, Scott Foresman (1986), Grade 3

The United States: Past to Present, D.C. Heath (1987), Grade 5

Focus on Earth Science,
Merrill (1987), Grade 9

Focus on Physical Science
Merrill (1987) Grade 9

Modern Biology, Holt, Rinehart
& Winston (1985), Grade 10

Land of Promise: A History of
the United States, Scott
Foresman (1987) Grade 10

United States History:
Reconstruction to the Present
Merrill (1986) Grade 10

Triumph of the American Nation
Harcourt, Brace, Javonovich
(1986), Grade 10

Designing the Textbook Appraisal Forms: The Theoretical Framework

Once the comprehensive review of the literature was complete, textbook appraisal forms were designed. They were intended to help the teacher appraisers assess "how" content is arranged and conveyed, and further assist them in identifying textbook design and strategies known to facilitate comprehension among students with low reading skills.

Constructionist, holistic models of learning guided the design of the appraisal forms. These theories represented a major shift in the way we had once thought about teaching the students with learning difficulties from the reductionist, differential diagnostic teaching models of the 1970's, to constructionist, schema and metacognitive theories which helped us understand the generative and cultural nature of language and reading development.

Schema Theory
Schema theory helps makes clear that comprehension is an active process which depends on a highly dynamic memory structure called schemata. Children with good reading skills "automatically" activate their "schemata" which exerts a strong influence on their ability to comprehend.

> Whether we are aware of it or not, it is the interaction of new information with the old knowledge that we mean when we use the term comprehension. To say that one has comprehended....is to say the he or she has found a "mental home" for the information ... or else that he or she has

> modified an existing mental home in order to accommodate new information.
>
> (Anderson & Pearson, 1980, p.225)

Evidence supports the notion that some students with poor reading skills can learn to activate their "schemata" particularly for comprehending and organizing text. Teaching techniques grounded in schema theory and designed to improve comprehension were identified and included:

- reciprocal teaching approaches that activate students' prior knowledge through explanations, instruction modelling and guided practice (Slavin, 1983; Palinscsar & Brown, 1988);

- presenting analogous information and inferential training (Hansen, 1981; Hansen & Pearson, 1983);

- using graphic organizers or displays to help students see links between old and new information, relationships among words and phrases (Johnston & Pearson, 1984; Flood & Lapp,1988)

- use of simulations, demonstrations and hands-on learning that serve to tap prior knowledge and motivation simultaneously (Foster, 1985; Lang, 1986).

Metacognitive Theory

Metacognitive theory describes how learning is regulated through functions of planning, checking and evaluating. Flavell (1976), a pioneer of the study of metacognition writes:

> Metacognition refers to one's knowledge concerning one's own cognitive processes.... for example, I am engaging in metacognition if I know I am having more trouble learning A than B, or if it strikes me that I should "double check" C before accepting it as a fact.
>
> (1976, p.232.)

Two metacognitive functions are necessary to be successful in reading: comprehension monitoring, and hypothesis formation evaluation. Evidence suggests that poor readers can be taught how to self-monitor while reading so they can take remedial action when they are confused or in doubt (Palincsar & Brown, 1984). Other researchers have been successful in teaching readers to use cues in the text to generate, evaluate and revise hypotheses about what they are reading (Idol, 1987).

Teaching techniques designed to improve metacognitive functions included:

- teaching students self-questioning procedures to use while reading (Alley & Hori, 1981; Wong & Jones, 1981);

- teaching students how to become more sensitive to text structures and other features in the text that signal important information (Gold & Fleisher, 1986; Smith & Friend, 1986; Anderson, Osborn & Tierney, 1984);

- providing students with guided pre-reading and guided reading techniques such as advanced organizers, mapping exercises or study guides (Armbruster, 1980; Bergerud, Lovitt & Horton, 1988; Flood, 1986; Idol, 1987).

What emerged was a 32-page, 200-question appraisal form based upon the notion that textbook teaching and learning have three interrelated and generative phases:

Phase I)   Getting students ready to learn;

Phase II)   actively engaging students in the reading and thinking activity; and

Phase III)   helping students extend their textbook knowledge.

References

Alley, G.R. & Hori, A.K. (1981). Effects of teaching a questioning strategy on reading comprehension of learning disabled adolescents. *Institute for Research in Learning Disabilities. Research Report #52.* Lawrence, Kansas: University of Kansas.

Alvermann, D.E., Smith, L.C., & Readence, J.E. (1985). Prior knowledge activation and the comprehension of compatible and incompatible text. *Reading Research Quarterly,* 20, (4), 420- 436.

Anderson, R.C. Osborne, J., & Tierney, R.J.,Eds.(1984) *Learning to Read in American Schools: Basal Readers and Content Texts.* Hillsdale, NJ: Erlbaum.

Anderson, R.C., & Pearson, P.D. (1980). A schema theoretical view of basic processes in reading comprehension. In R. Spiro, B. Bruce and W. Brewer (Eds.), *Theoretical Issues in Reading Comprehension.* Hillsdale, NJ: Erlbaum.

Anderson, T.H. & Armbruster, B.B. (1984). Content area textbooks. In R.C. Anderson, J. Osborne and R.J. Tierney, (Eds.), *Learning to Read in American Schools.* Hillsdale, NJ: Erlbaum.

Armbruster, B.B. (1980). Mapping: An innovative reading and comprehension study strategy. Paper presented at the Annual Meeting of the American Educational Research Association, Boston, MA.

Armbruster, B.B. & Anderson, T.H. (1988). On selecting "considerate content area textbooks." *Remedial and Special Education,* 9, 1, 47-52.

Armbruster, B.B. & Gudbrandsen, B. (1986) Reading comprehension in social studies programs. *Reading Research Quarterly,* 21, 36-48.

Armbruster, B.B., Osborne, J.H., & Davison, A.L. (1985). Readability formulas may be dangerous to your textbooks. *Educational Leadership*, 42, 18-20.

Bartnick, W.M., & Parkay, F.W. (1991). A comparative analysis of the "holding power" of general and exceptional education programs. *Remedial and Special Education*, 12, 5, 17-22.

Bergerud, D., Lovitt, T.C., & Horton, S. (1988). The effectiveness of textbook adaptations in life science for high school students with learning disabilities. *Journal of Learning Disabilities*, 21, 2, 70-76.

Berkowitz, S.J. (1986). Effects of instruction in text organization on 6th grade students' memory for expository reading. *Reading Research Quarterly*, 21, 161-178.

Bloomer, R., Bates, H., Brown, S., & Norlander K. (1982). *Mainstreaming in Vermont: a Study of the Identification Process*. Livonia, N.Y.: Brador Publications.

Britton, B. (1988). The impact of good and bad writers on learners. Paper presented at the Annual Meeting of the American Educational Research Association, New Orleans.

Bruce, M.E. & Chan, L.K.S. (1991). Reciprocal teaching and transenvironmental programming. *Remedial and Special Education*, 12, 5, 44-55.

Chall, J.S. (1983). *Learning to Read: The Great Debate*. New York: McGraw-Hill.

Chall, J.S. & Conard, S.S. (1991). *Should Textbooks Challenge Students?* New York, NY: Teachers College Press.

Chall, J.S., Conard, S. & Harris, S. (1977). An analysis of textbooks in relation to declining SAT scores. Princeton,

NJ: College Entrance Examination Board, and Educational Testing Service.

Ciborowski, J., Antes, M.M., Zorfass, J.M., & Ames, N. (1989). Improving textbooks and teacher's editions to meet the needs of diverse students. *Book Research Quarterly*, 5,3, 75-90.

Deshler, D.D., & Schumaker, J.B. (1986). Learning strategies: An instructional alternative for low-achieving adolescents. Exceptional Children, 52, 583-590.

Education Developmental Center and RMC Research. (1989). *Improving Textbook Usability:* final report (ERIC Document Reproduction Service, no. ED 310585).

Ellis, E.S., Deshler, D.D., Lenz, E.K., Schumaker, J.B., Clark, F.L. (1991). An instructional model for teaching learning strategies. *Focus on Exceptional Children*, 23, 6, 1-24.

Ensminger, E.E. & Dangel, H.L. (1992). The Foxfire pedagogy: a confluence of best practices for special education. *Focus on Exceptional Children*, 24, 7, 1-15.

Fiore, T.A., Danin, S.T., & Nero, R.C. (1992). *Textbook Adoption Processes and Criteria and the Implications for Integrating Children with Disabilities into Mainstream Education.* Final Technical Report. Research Triangle Institute.

Flavell, J.H. (1976). Metacognitive aspects of problem solving. In L.B. Resnick (Ed.), *The Nature of Intelligence.* Hillsdale, NJ: Erlbaum.

Flood, J. (1986). The text, the student and the teacher: learning from exposition in middle schools. *The Reading Teacher*, April, 785-790.

Flood, J. & Lapp, D. (1988). Conceptual mapping startegies for understanding information texts. *The Reading Teacher*, 41, 8, 780-783.

Foster, J. (1985). *Adaptation of Instructional Materials for use with Mainstreamed Students.* Cambridge, MA.: Technical Education Research Center.

Fourqurean, J.M. & LaCourt, T. (1990). A follow-up of former special education students: a model for program evaluation. *Remedial and Special Education*, 12, (1), 16-22.

Gagnon, P. (1987). Democracy's untold story, *American Educator*, 11, 2, 19-25.

Gaskins, I. & Elliot, T. (1991). *Implementing Cognitive Strategy Training Across the School.* Cambridge, MA: Brookline Books.

Gee, T.C. & Forester, N. (1988). Moving reading beyond the reading classroom. *Journal of Reading*, 31, 505-511.

Gold, J. & Fleisher, L.S. (1986). Comprehension breakdown with inductively organized text: differences between average and disabled readers. *Remedial and Special Education*, 7, 4, 26-32.

Goodlad, J.I. (1976). *Facing The Future: Issues in Education and Schooling.* New York: McGraw-Hill.

Hansen, J. (1981). The effects of inference training and practice on young children's reading comprehension. *Reading Research Quarterly*, 3, 391-417.

Hansen, J. & Pearson, D.P. (1983). An instructional study: Improving the inferential comprehension of good and poor fourth grade readers. *Journal of Educational Psychology*, 75, 6, 821- 829.

Harris, K. R. & Pressley, M. (1991) The nature of cognitive strategy instruction: interactive strategy construction. *Exceptional Children, 57,* 392-404.

Haskell, D.W., Foorman, B.R., & Swank, P.R. (1992). Effects of three orthographic/phonological units on first grade reading. *Remedial and Special Education*, 13, 2, 40-49.

Herber, H.L. (1978). *Teaching Reading in the Content Areas.* Englewood Cliffs, NJ.: Prentice Hall.

Idol, L. (1987). A critical thinking map to improve content area comprehension of poor readers. *Remedial and Special Education*, 8,4, 28-40.

Idol, L. (1988). Johnny can't read: does the fault lie with the book, the teacher or Johnny? *Remedial and Special Education*, 9,1, 25-35.

Idol, L., West, F. & Lloyd, S. (1988). Organizing and implementing specialized reading programs: A collaborative approach involving classroom, remedial and special education teachers. *Remedial and Special Education*, 9, 2, 54-61.

Irwin, J.L. (1989). *Reading and the Middle School Student: Strategies to Enhance Literacy.* Boston, MA.: Allyn and Bacon.

Johnston, P. & Pearson, P.D. (1984). *Prior Knowledge, Connectivity and the Assessment of Reading Comprehension.* Technical Report #245. Urbana: University of Illinois, Center for the Study of Reading.

Larkins, G.A. & Hawkins, M.L. (1987). Trivial and noninformative content of social studies textbooks in the primary grades. Paper presented at American Educational Research Association, April, 1987.

Loman, N.L. & Mayer, R.E. (1983). Signaling techniques that increase the understanding of expository prose. *Journal of Educational Psychology*, 75, 402-412.

Lovitt, T.C. & Horton, S.V. (1991). Adapting textbooks for mildly handicapped adolescents. In G. Stoner, M.

Shinn & H. Walker (Eds.), *Intervention for Achievement and Behavior Problems*. NASP Monographs.

Lunstrum, J.P. & Taylor, B.L. (1980). *Teaching Reading in the Social Studies*, Newark, DE: International Reading Association.

McGill-Franzen, A. & Allington, R.L. (1991). The gridlock of low reading achievement: Perspectives on practice and policy,. *Remedial and Special Education*, 12, 3, 20-30.

Moore, D.W., Readence, J.E., & Rickleman, R.J. (1983). An historical explanation of content reading instruction, *Reading Research Quarterly*, 18, 419-438.

National Center for Educational Statistics (1989). Office of Educational Research and Improvement, Washington, D.C.

Palinscar, A.S. & Brown, A.L. (1984). Reciprocal teaching of comprehension-monitoring activities. *Cognition and Instruction*, 1,2, 117-175.

Palincsar, A.S. & Brown, A.L. (1986). Interactive teaching to promote independent learning from text. *The Reading Teacher*, 39, 771-777.

Palinscar, A.S. & Brown, A.L. (1988). Teaching and practicing thinking skills to promote comprehension in the context of group problem solving. *Remedial and Special Education*, 9, 1, 53-59.

Poplin, M.S. (1988) The reductionist fallacy in learning disabilities: replicating the past by reducing the present. *Journal of Learning Disabilities*, 21, 389-400.

Pressley, M., Burkell, J., Cariglia-Bull, T., Lysynchuk, L., McGoldrick, J.A., Schneider, B., Snyder, B.L., Symons, S., Woloshyn, V.E. (1990). *Cognitive Strategy Instruction That Really Improves Children's Academic Performance*.

Cambridge, MA: Brookline Books.

Pressley, M., El-Dinary, P.B., Gaskins, I., Schuder, T., Bergman, J.L., Almasi, J., & Brown, R. (1992) Beyond direct explanation: Transactional instruction of reading comprehension strategies. *Elementary School Journal, 92,* 511-554.

Readence, J.E., Bean, T.W., & Baldwin, R.S. (1981). *Content Area Reading: An Integrated Approach.* Dubuque, IA.: Kendall/Hunt.

Reynolds, M.C., Wang, M.C., & Walberg, H. (1987). The necessary restructuring of special and regular education. *Exceptional Children,* 53, 391-398.

Santa, C.M. & Alvermann, D.E. (1991). *Science Learning: Processes and Applications.* Newark, DE.: International Reading Association.

Scruggs, T., Mastropieri, M., Levin, J., Mcloone, B., Gaffney, J., & Prater, M. (1985). Increasing content-area learning: A comparison of mnemonic and visual-spatial direct instruction. *Learning Disabilities Research,* 1, 1, 22.

Slavin, R.E. (1983). *Cooperative Learning.* New York: Longman.

Slavin, R.E., Karweit, N.L., & Madden, N.A. (1989). *Effective Programs for Students at Risk.* Boston, MA.: Allyn & Bacon.

Smith, P.L. & Friend, M. (1986). Training learning disabled adolescents in a strategy for using text structures to aid recall of instructional prose. *Learning Disability Research,* 2, 1, 38-44.

Snider, V.E. & Tarver, S.G. (1987). The effect of early reading failure on acquisition of prior knowledge among students with learning disabilities. *Journal of Learning Disabilities,* 20 (6), 351-356.

Stainback, S. & Stainback, W. (1987). Integration versus coop-
eration: A commentary on educating children with
learning problems: A shared responsibility. *Exceptional Children*, 66-68.

Stanovich, K. (1986a). Matthew effects in reading: Some conse-
quences of individual differences in the acquisition of
literacy. *Reading Research Quarterly*, 21 (4), 360-407.

Stanovich, K. (1986). Cognitive processes and the reading problems of learning disabled children: Evaluating the assumptions of specificity. In J.K. Torgesen and B.Y.L.
Wong (Eds.),*Psychological and Educational Perspectives
on Learning Disabilities*, Orlando, Fl.: Academic Press.

Swanson, H.L. (1989). Strategy instruction: Overview of principles and procedures for effective use. *Learning Disability Quarterly*, 12, 1, 3-16.

Thorndyke, P.W. (1977). Cognitive structures in comprehension and memory of narrative discourse. *Cognitive
Psychology*, 9, 113-126.

Thrope, L.D. (1986). *Prior knowledge and reading: An investigation
of fourth and fifth grade social studies and science readers*.
Unpublished dissertation, San Diego State University
and Claremont Graduate School.

Tyson-Bernstein, H. (1988). *A Conspiracy of Good Intentions:
America's Textbook Fiasco*. Washington D.C.: Council
for Basic Education.

Tyson-Bernstein, H. & Woodward, A. (1989). Why students
aren't learning very much from their textbooks. *Educational Leadership*, 47, 3, 14-17.

U.S. Department of Education, (1991). *Thirteenth Annual Report
to Congress on the Implementation of the Individuals With
Disabilities Education Act*. Washington, D.C.

Vacca, R.T. (1981). *Content Area Reading*. Boston, MA.: Little, Brown Co.

Vaughn, J.L., & Estes, T.H. (1986). *Reading and Reasoning Beyond the Primary Grades*. Boston, MA.: Allyn & Bacon.

Vellutino, F. (1991). Introduction to three studies on reading acquisition: Convergent findings on theoretcial foundations of code-oriented versus whole-language approaches to reading instruction. *Journal of Educational Psychology*, 83, 4, 437-433.

Will, M. (1986). Educating students with learning problems - a shared responsibility. *Exceptional Children*, 52, 5, 411-415.

Wolman, C., Bruininks, R., & Thurlow, M.L. (1989). Dropouts and dropout programs: Implications for special education. *Remedial and Special Education*, 10, 5, 6-20.

Woodward, A., & Elliott, D.L. (1990). Textbook use and teacher professionalism. In D.L. Elliott & A. Woodward (Eds.), *Textbooks and Schooling in the U.S.* (89th Yearbook of the National Society for the Study of Education, Part 1, pp. 178-193). Chicago: National Society for the Study of Education.

Wong, B.Y.L. & Jones, W. (1981). *Increasing metacomprehension in learning disabled and normally-achieving students through self-questioning training*. Unpublished manuscript, Simon Fraser University.

Wong, B.Y.L. (1985). Issues in cognitive behavioral intervention in academic skill areas. *Journal of Abnormal Child Psychology*,2, 123-131.

Zigmond, N. (1990). Rethinking secondary school programs for students with learning disabilities. *Focus on Exceptional Children*, 23, 1, 1-22.

Index